My Alphabet Tracing Expedition

READY FOR TAKE-OFF!

Hey Awesome Parents!

Welcome to My Alphabet Tracing Expedition!

We're passionate about making learning fun! This book is packed with prompts to spark imagination, build vocabulary and develop fine motor skills through tracing.

Spark Creativity Together!

- Read the prompts together, encouraging your child to imagine and repeat.
- Celebrate squiggly mistakes - they're part of the learning process!
- Coloring pages let them unleash creativity while learning fun facts.
- Complete the learning journey with a celebratory "Tracing Champion" certificate!

You're Your Child's First Alphabet Coach! We wish you a joy-filled learning adventure!

Positive reviews from awesome parents like you help others discover this book! Share your experience to help other families create happy learning memories.

Copyright © 2024 The Spark Foundry. All rights reserved.

No portion of this book may be reproduced, distributed or transmitted in any form or by any means, including photocopying, recording, or other electronic or mechanical methods, without the prior written permission of the publisher.

Trace the Amazing A

<u>A</u>li, the <u>a</u>stronaut is looking for an <u>a</u>mazing <u>a</u>dventure! Let's trace 'A' to make an <u>a</u>irplane that will fly <u>A</u>li to <u>A</u>ntarctica.

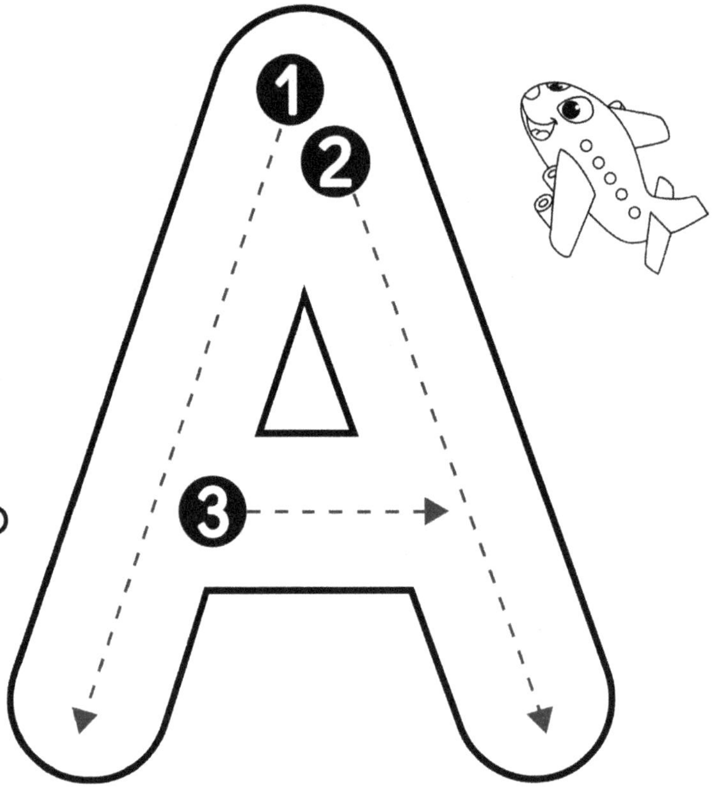

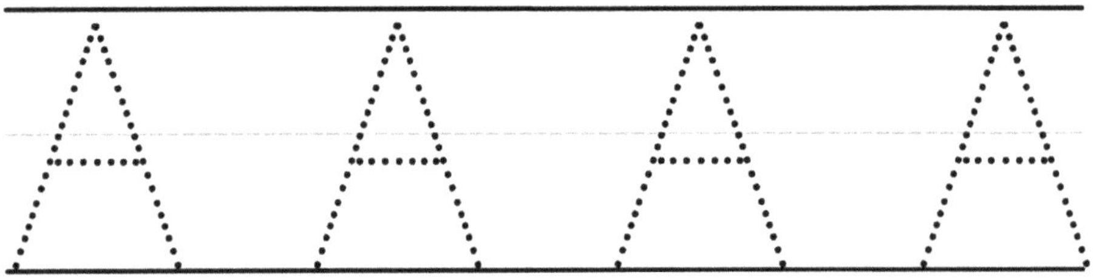

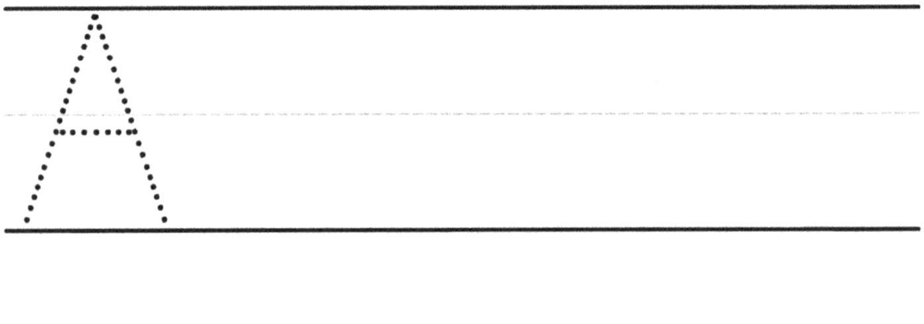

Trace the small alphabet

Awesome! You <u>a</u>ced that A! Now, let's trace this small 'a' and see what tiny <u>a</u>nimal it can become.

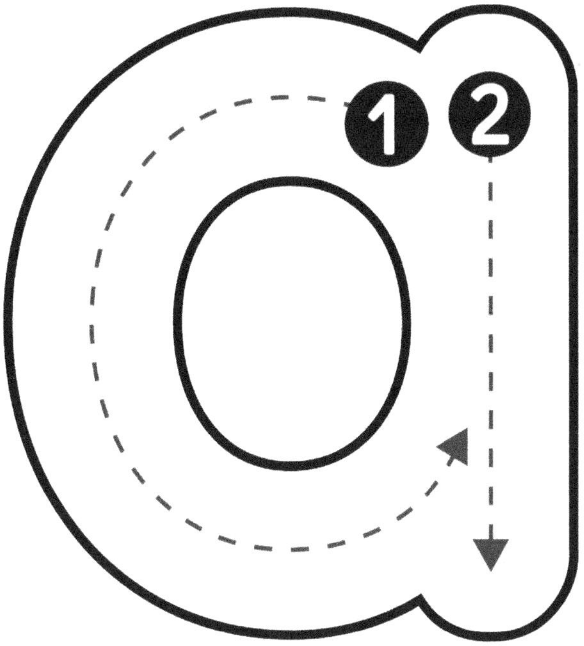

Ant

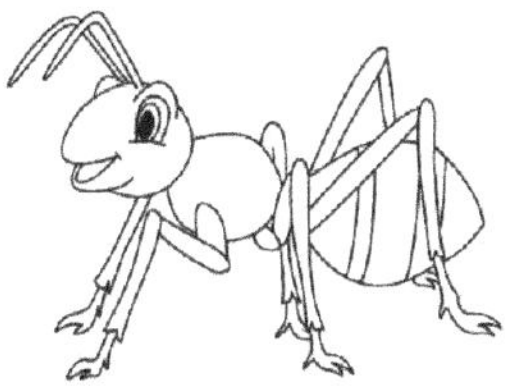

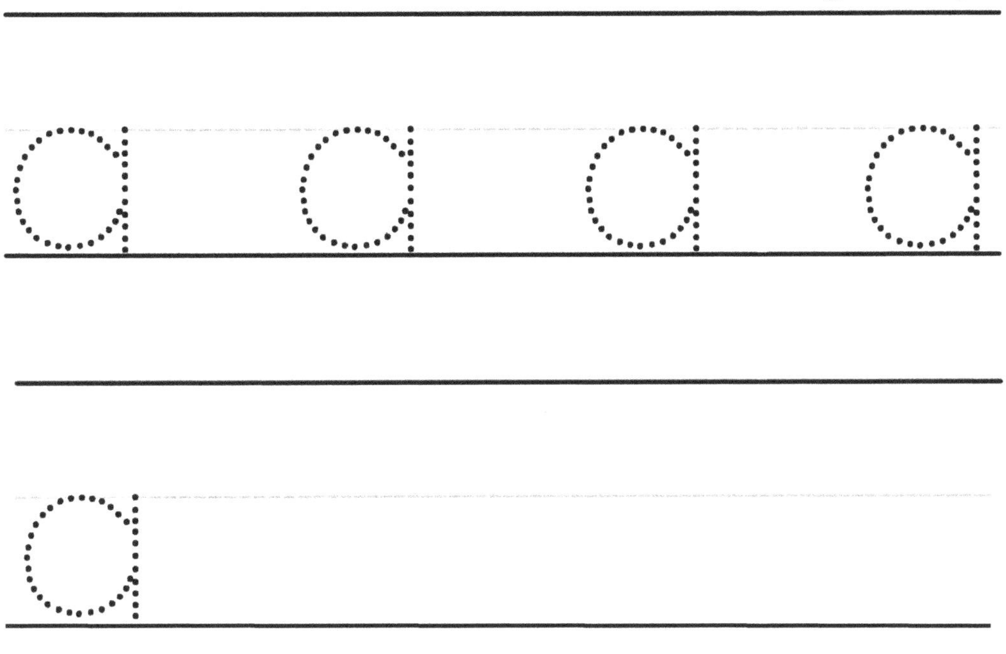

Time to Practice

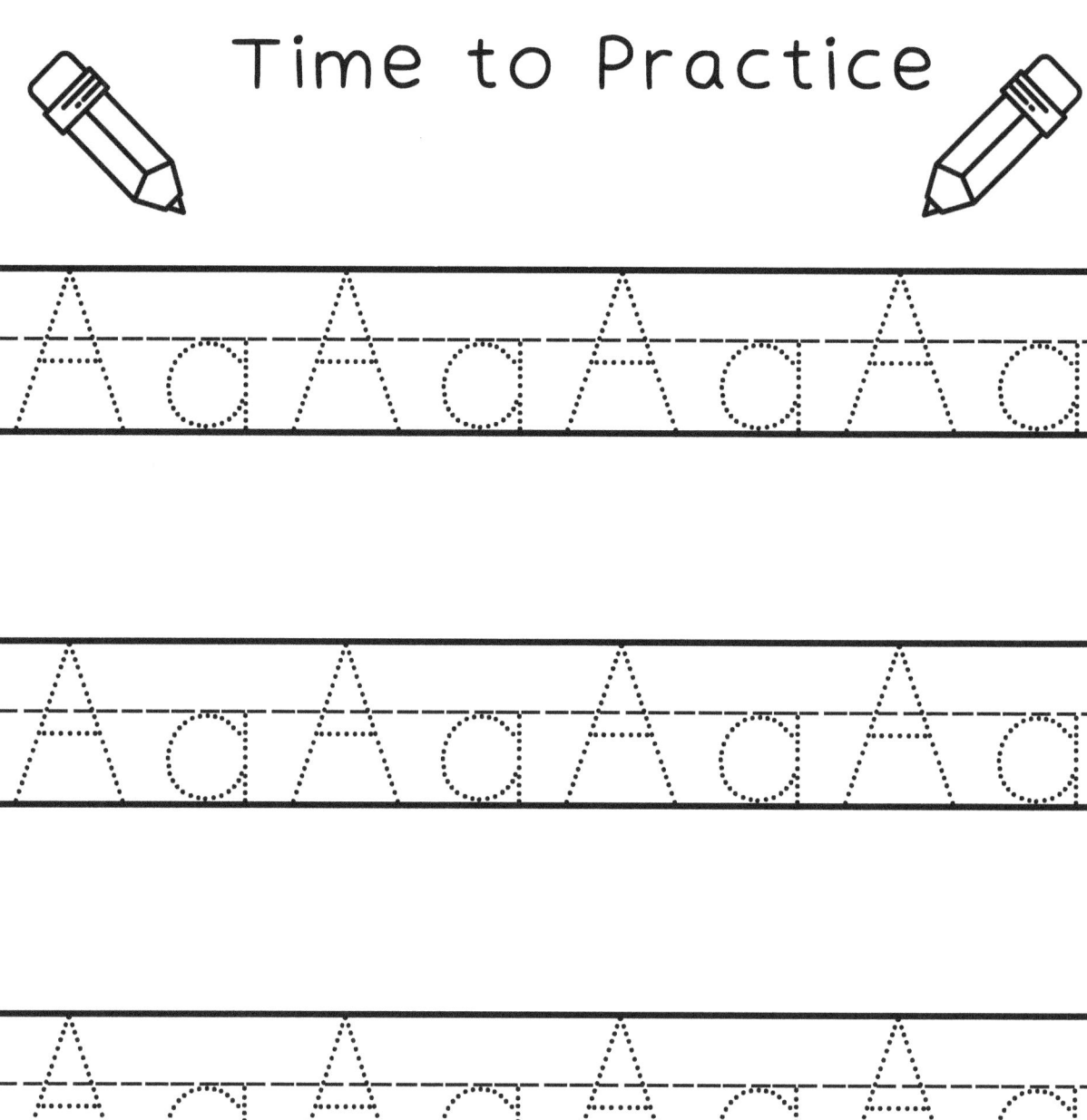

Color Me FUN!

 Wow! You're <u>a</u>mazing. Tracing the 'A' was super fun! Are you ready to color the <u>a</u>dorable <u>A</u>lpaca?

A is for Alpaca

Did you know? Alpacas are super fluffy friends! Their fur is even softer than a sheep's wool!

Trace the Big B

The <u>b</u>ig <u>b</u>lue <u>b</u>ird sings a happy song sitting on top of his <u>b</u>irdhouse. Can you trace it to make it the <u>b</u>est 'B' ever?

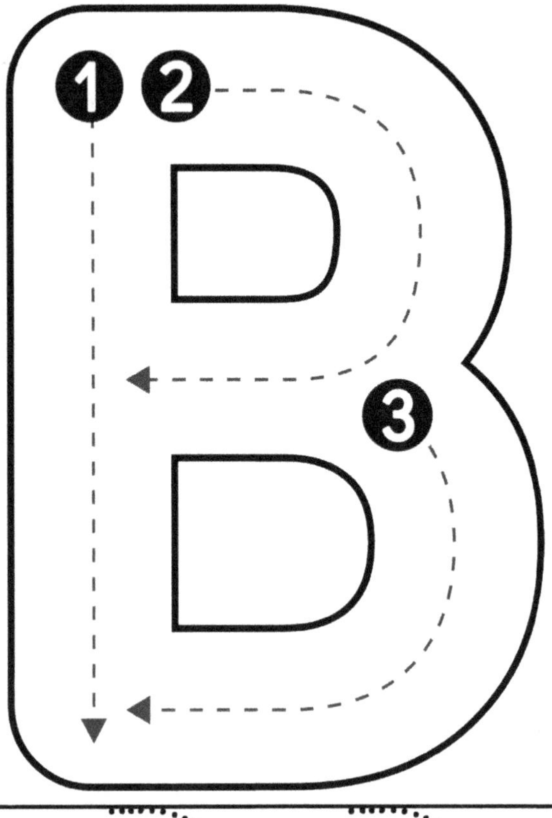

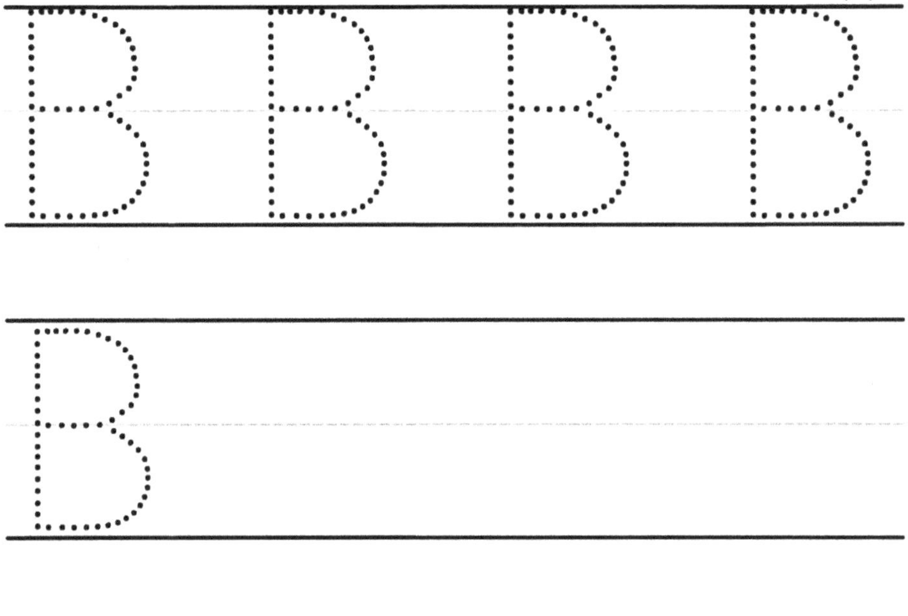

Trace the small alphabet

You are doing great! Trace the small 'b' and turn it into a <u>b</u>eautiful <u>b</u>utterfly.

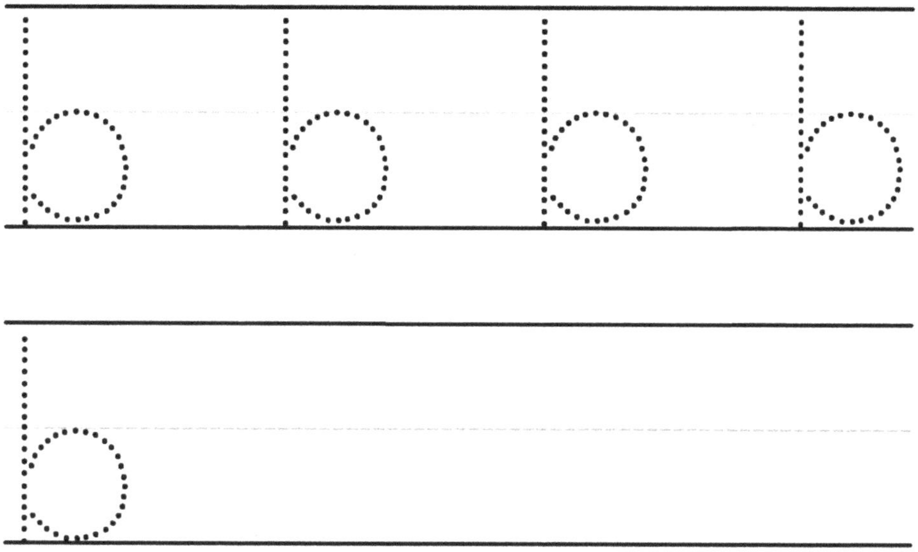

Time to Practice

Color Me FUN!

You traced 'B' brilliantly! Now, Let's color the busy, bees! Can you make a buzzing sound like the bees?

B is for Bee

Did you know? Bees fly from flower to flower sipping sweet flower juice called nectar. Then, they turn that nectar into yummy honey that we love to eat!

Trace the cool C

The cool, curvy 'C' is super fun to trace! Maybe it will turn into a bumpy camel when we're done!

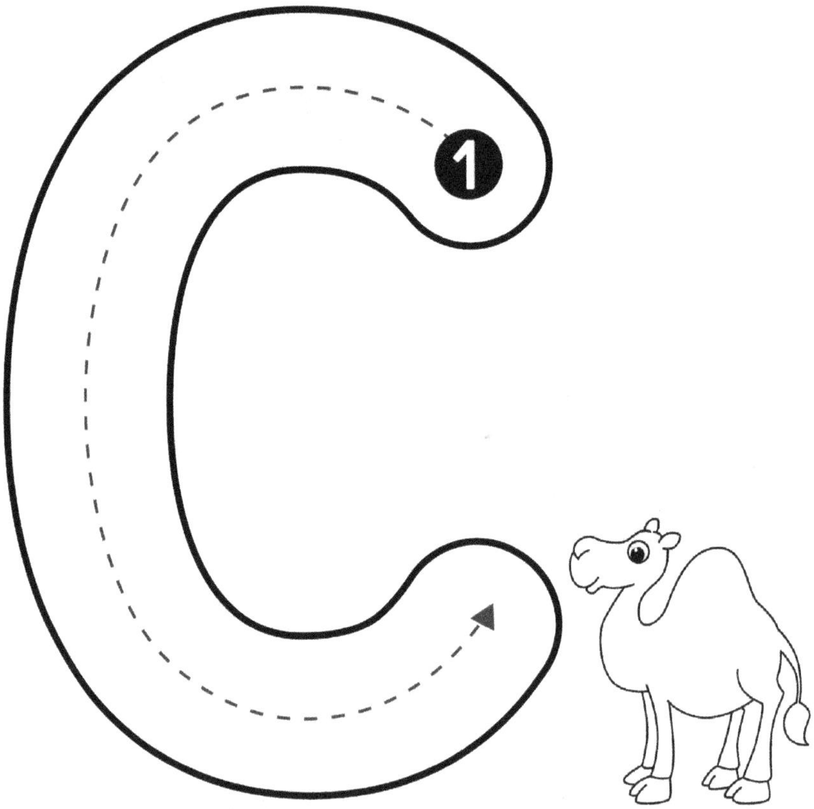

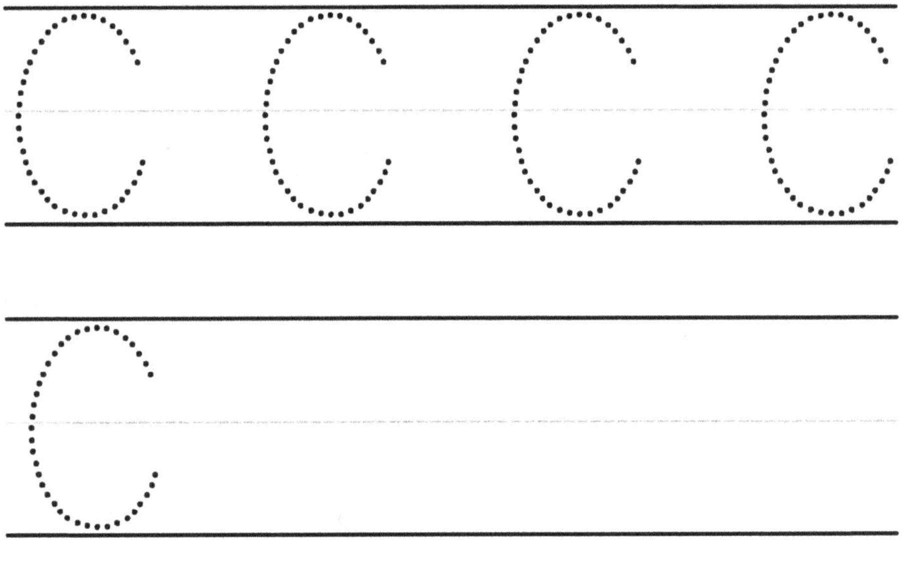

Trace the small alphabet

LOOK at that small 'c'! Let's trace it carefully so it can become a cute cat.

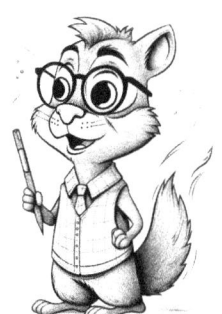

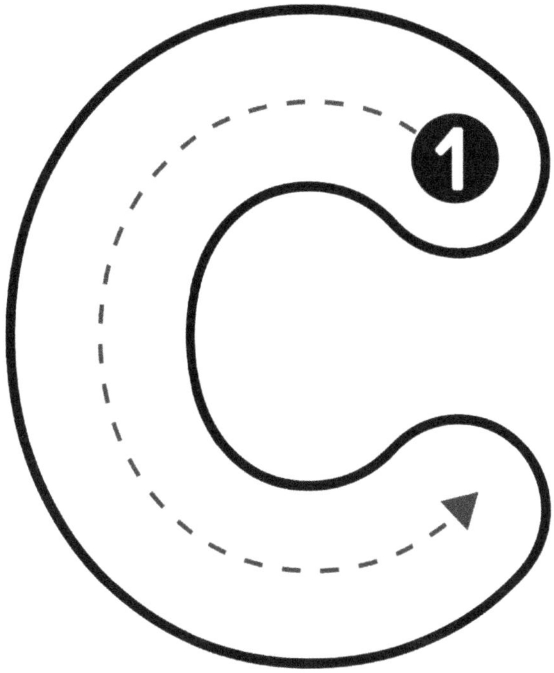

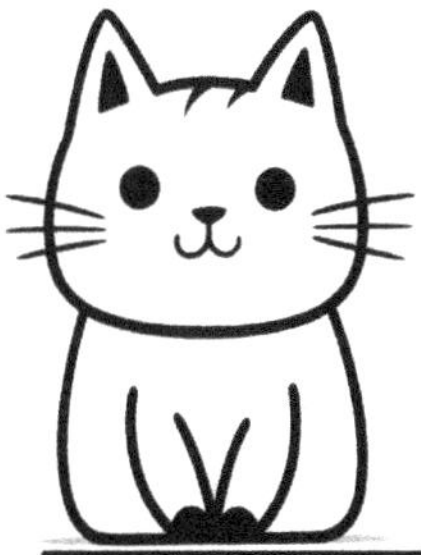

c c c c

c

 # Time to Practice

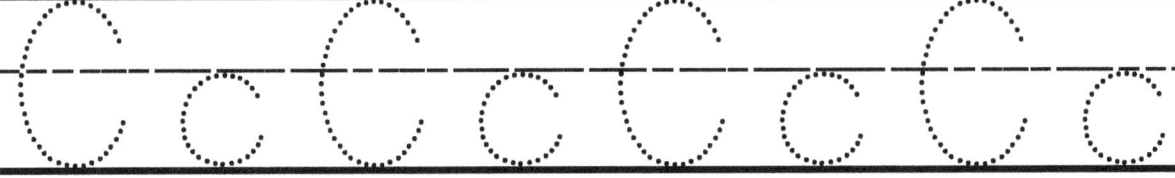

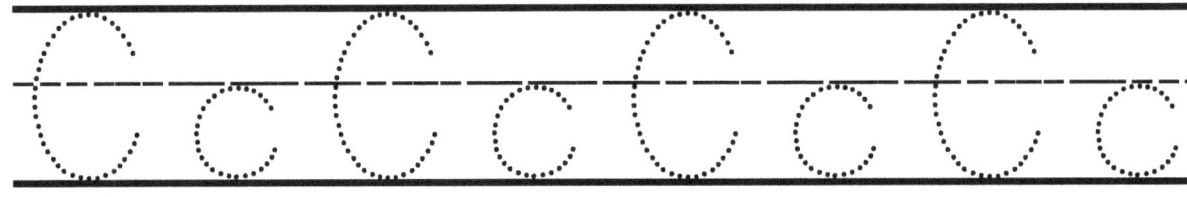

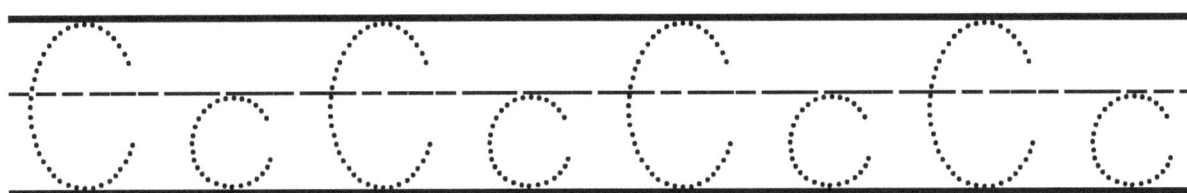

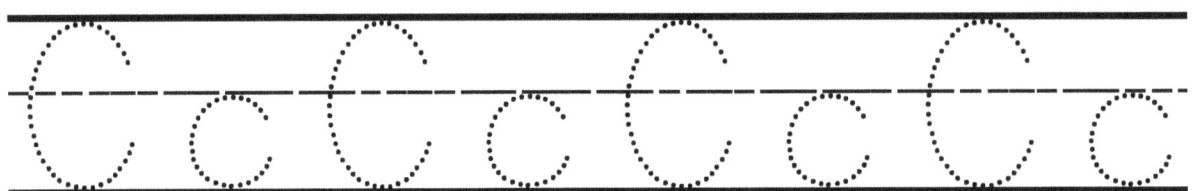

Color Me FUN!

You are a tracing <u>c</u>hampion! Let's <u>c</u>olor this <u>c</u>hicken and make it the happiest bird in the <u>c</u>oop!

C is for Chicken

Did you know? Chickens love to cluck and scratch the ground! They're looking for yummy worms and seeds to eat.

Trace the Dancing D

Let's trace this dancing 'D' and turn it into <u>d</u>elicious <u>d</u>onut treats for <u>D</u>exter the <u>D</u>almatian!

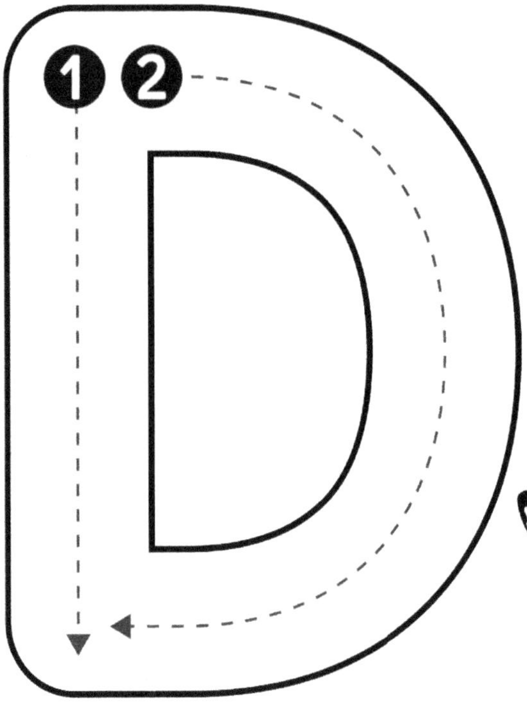

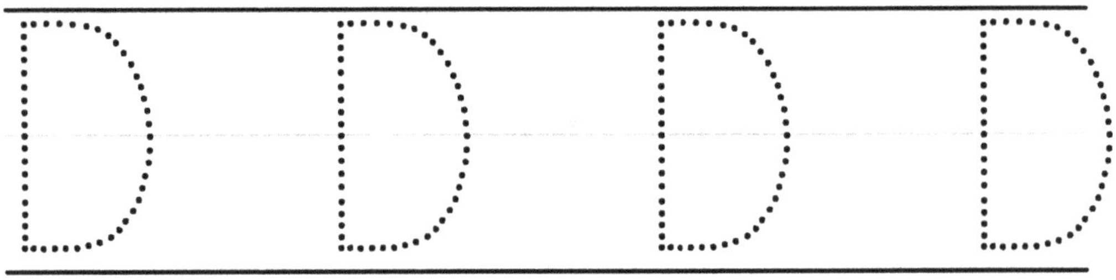

Trace the small alphabet

You are <u>d</u>oing great! Let's trace the small 'd' and make its <u>d</u>ream of becoming the <u>d</u>inasour come true!

Time to Practice

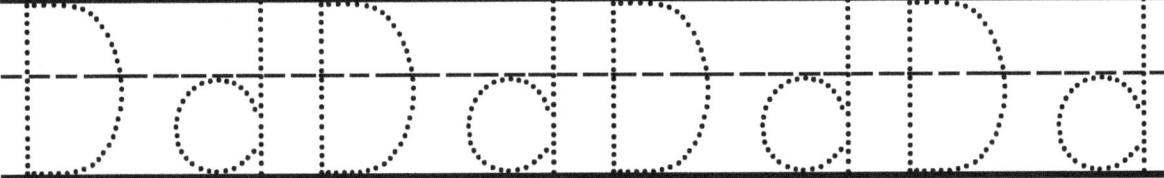
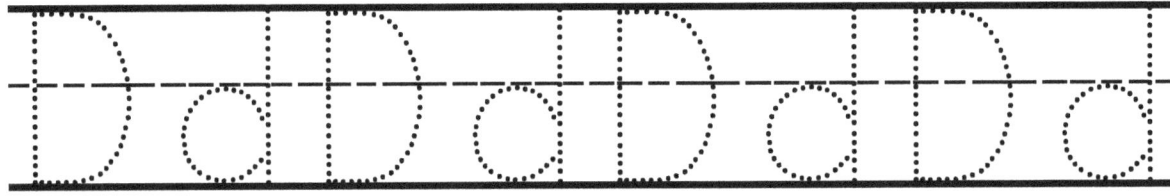

Color Me FUN!

<u>D</u>azzling job tracing! Time to color! Use your favorite colors to make the <u>d</u>olphin do a flip.

D is for Dolphin

Did you know? Dolphins are super smart! They can even call each other by name with special whistles!

Trace the Energetic E

Wow! You're tracing like an energetic eagle! Excellent work!

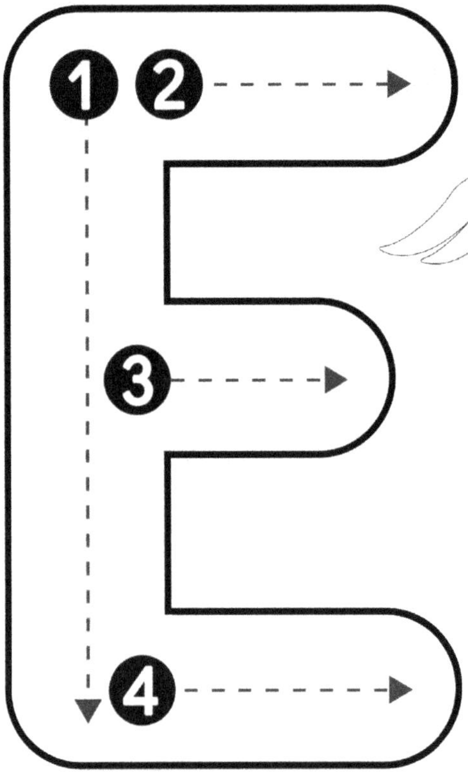

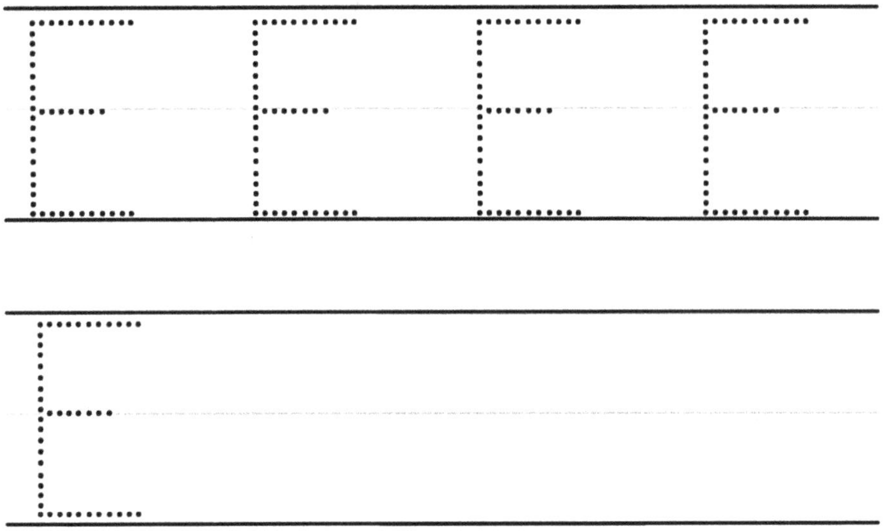

Trace the small alphabet

 Let's trace this small 'e' <u>e</u>xtra carefully! Once we're done, it will turn into an <u>ee</u>l ready to <u>e</u>xplore the ocean!

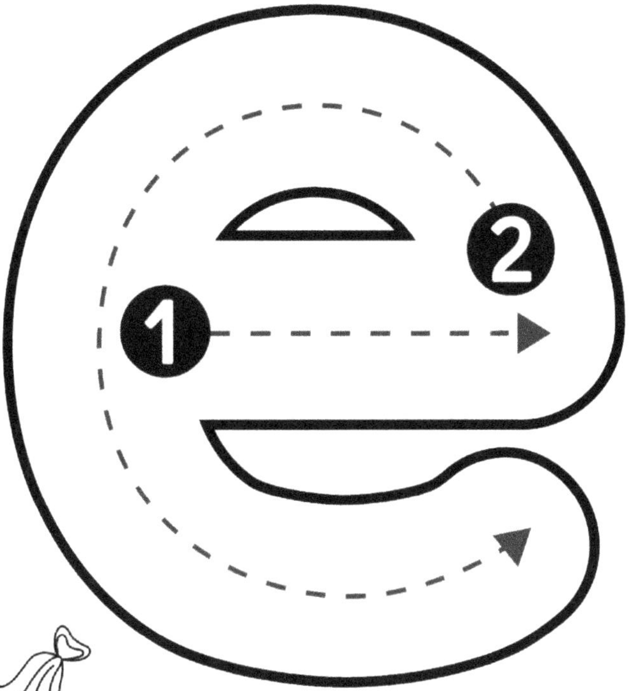

Time to Practice

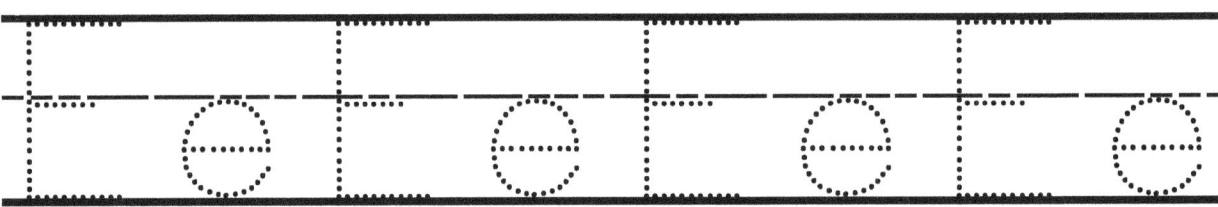

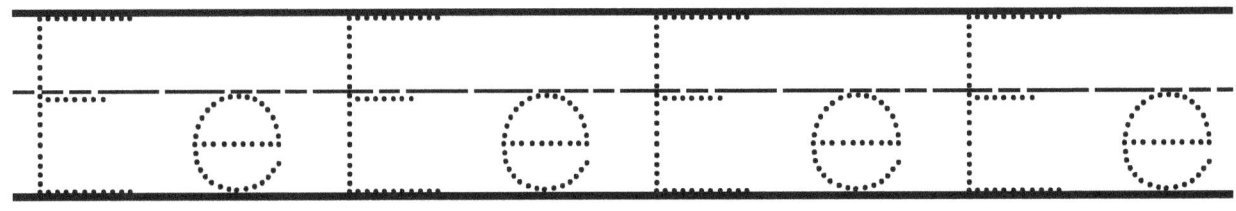

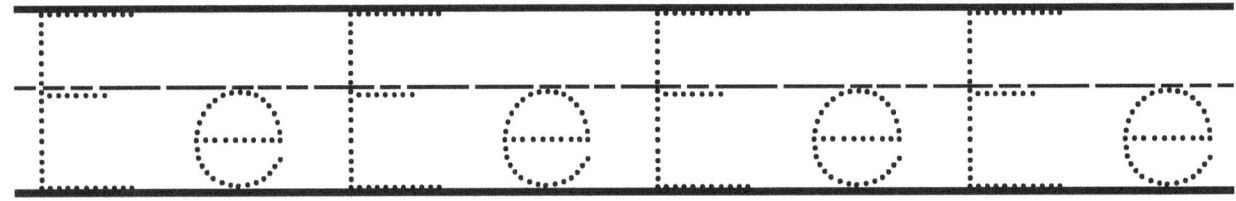

Color Me FUN!

Excellent job tracing that 'E'! Time to color these happy elephants with exciting colors! Don't forget their enormous ears!

E is for Elephant

Did you Know? Elephants are the BIGGEST land animals on Earth!

Trace the Funny F

Look a _f_unny _f_ace is sitting on top of a _f_lower. Let's trace the 'F' and see what it looks like!

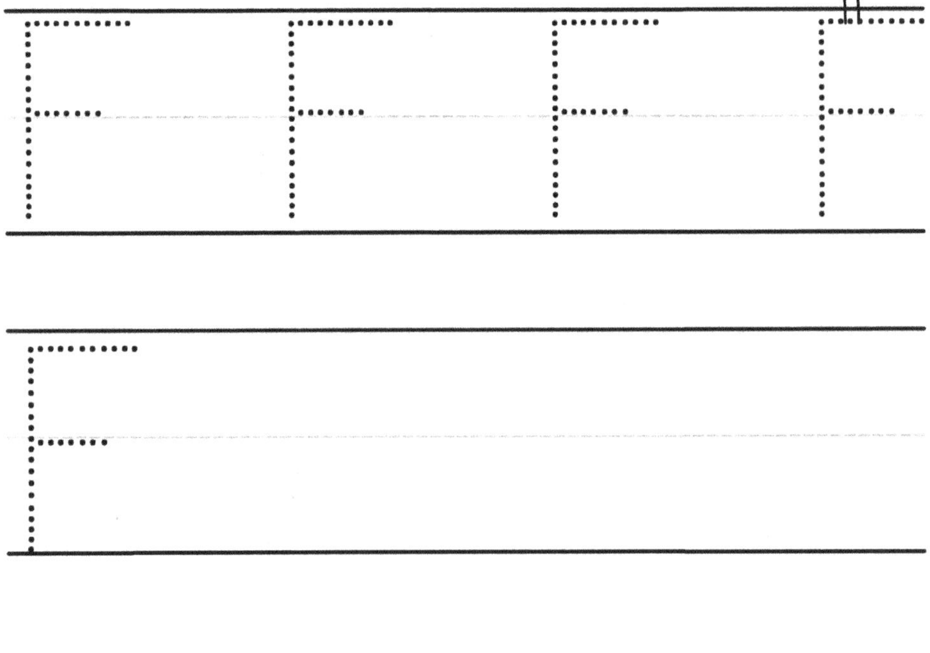

Trace the small alphabet

The small 'f' is <u>f</u>eeling good! Let's trace it <u>f</u>ast to turn our <u>f</u>riend, <u>F</u>urry the bunny into a <u>f</u>lower!

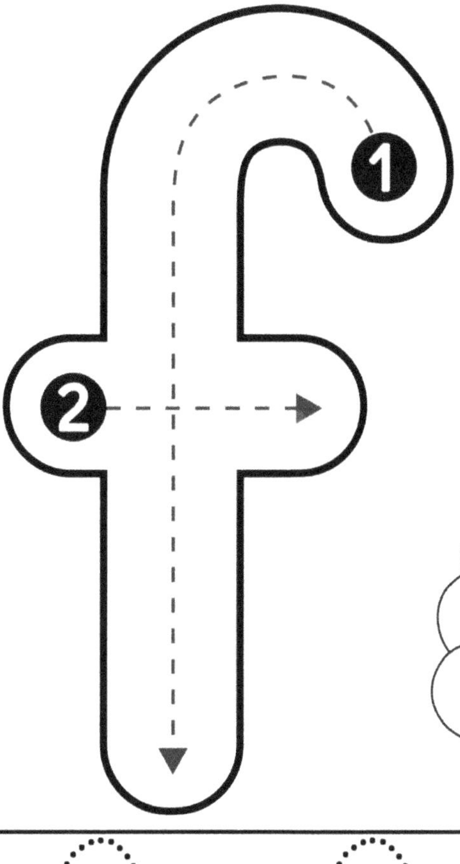

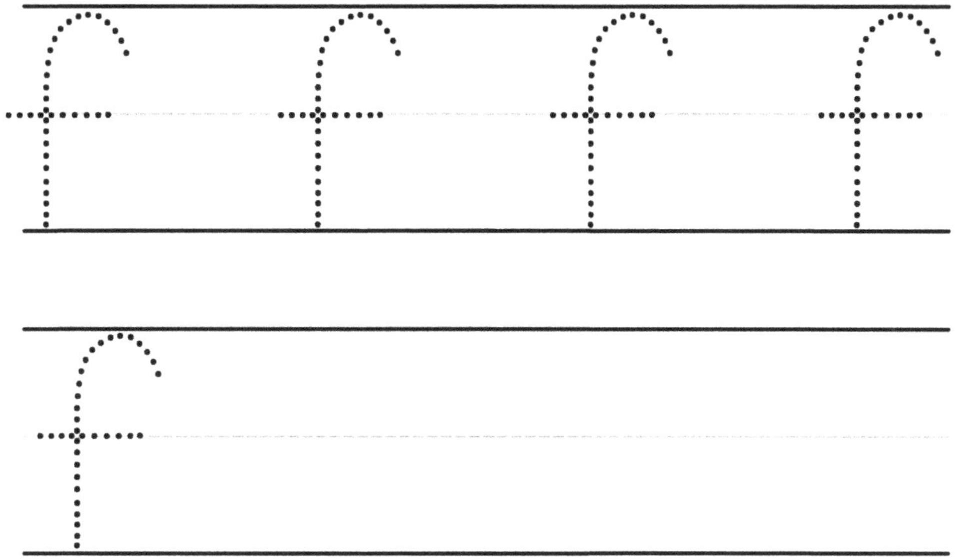

Time to Practice

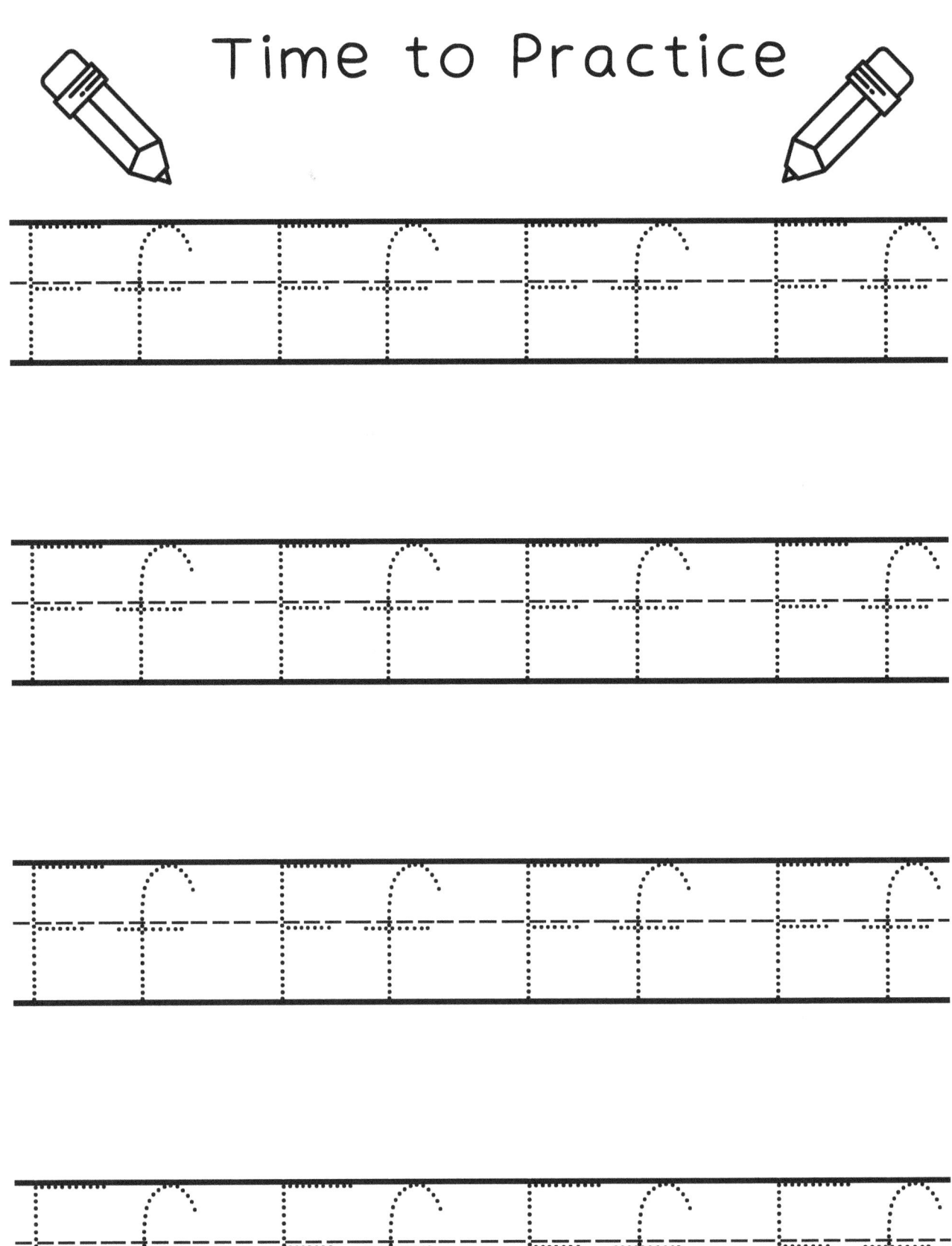

Color Me FUN!

<u>F</u>antastic work tracing 'F'. Let's have some <u>f</u>un coloring <u>F</u>roggie, the <u>f</u>rog with your <u>f</u>avorite color.

F is for Frog

Did you know? Frogs can jump really high and they like to eat bugs! What's your favorite yummy food?

Trace the Gigantic G

Ready, set, go! Let's trace the Gigantic 'G' with our silly goat!

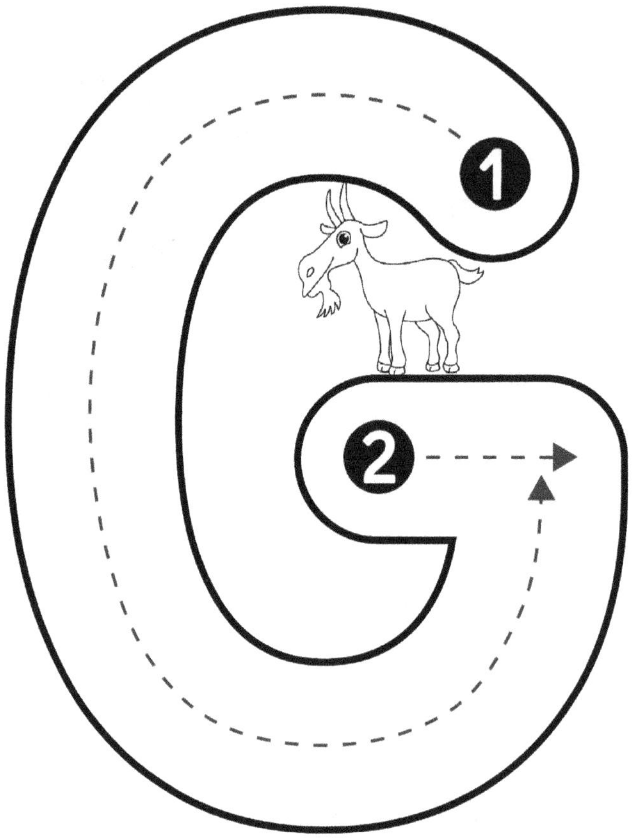

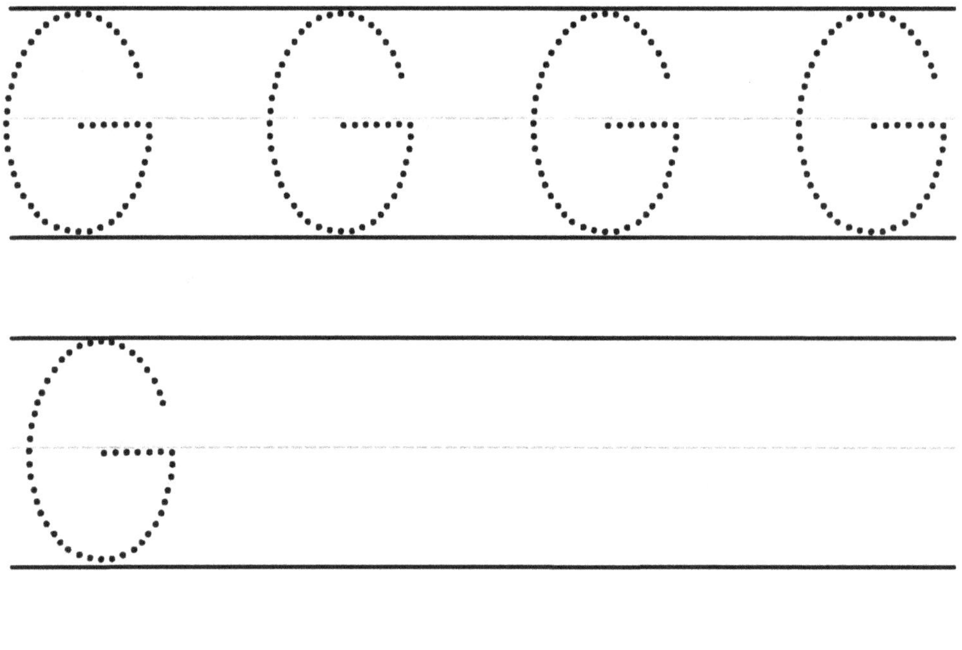

Trace the small alphabet

Giggle giggle 'g'! Let's trace it gently to peek what's inside the gift box!

Time to Practice

Color Me FUN!

You did a great job tracing the '<u>G</u>'. Th$\overline{is}$ giant g$\overline{o}$rilla is ready for s$\overline{ome}$ c$\overline{ol}\overline{o}$rful fun!

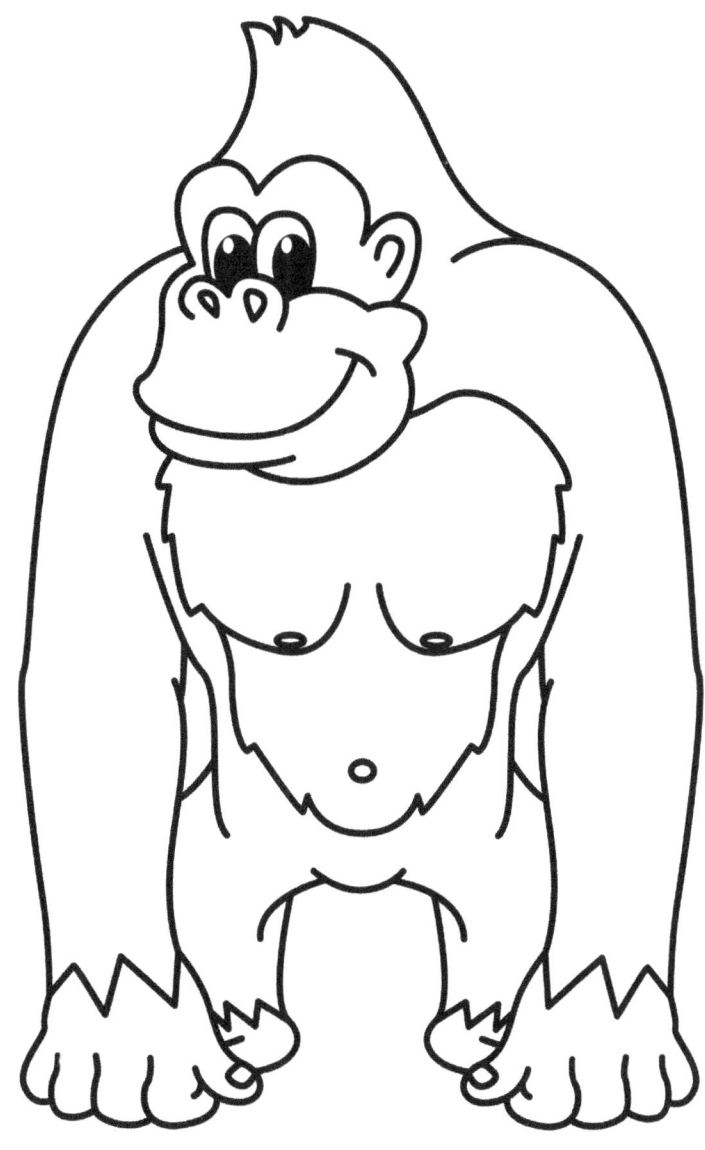

G is for Gorilla

Did you Know? Gorillas are really strong!
Strong enough to carry a big tree!

Trace the Hopping H

Let's say <u>h</u>ooray, tracing the <u>h</u>opping 'h' with a <u>h</u>appy face!

Trace the small alphabet

Let's trace the small <u>h</u>andsome 'h' and build a <u>h</u>ouse next it.

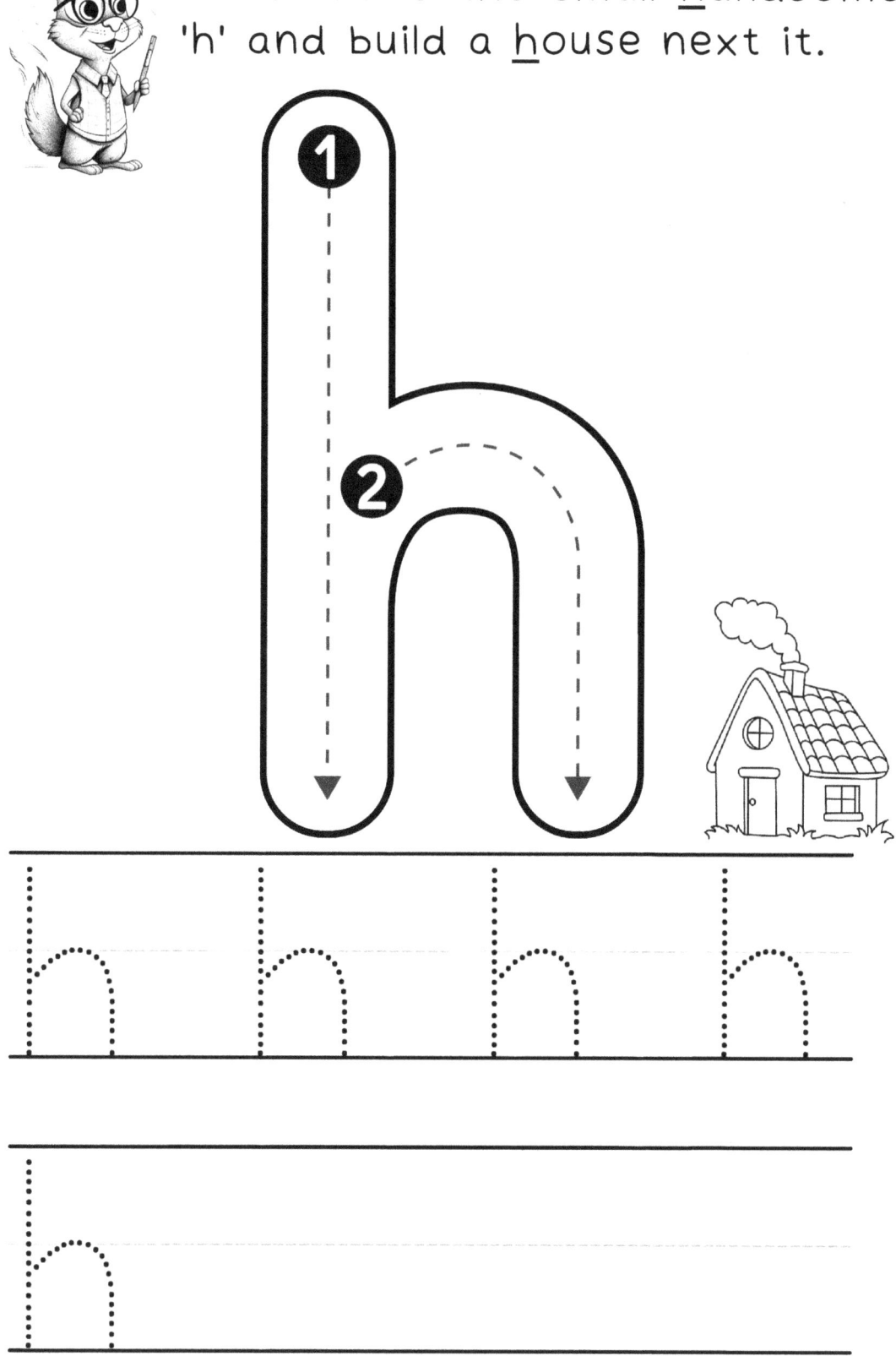

Time to Practice

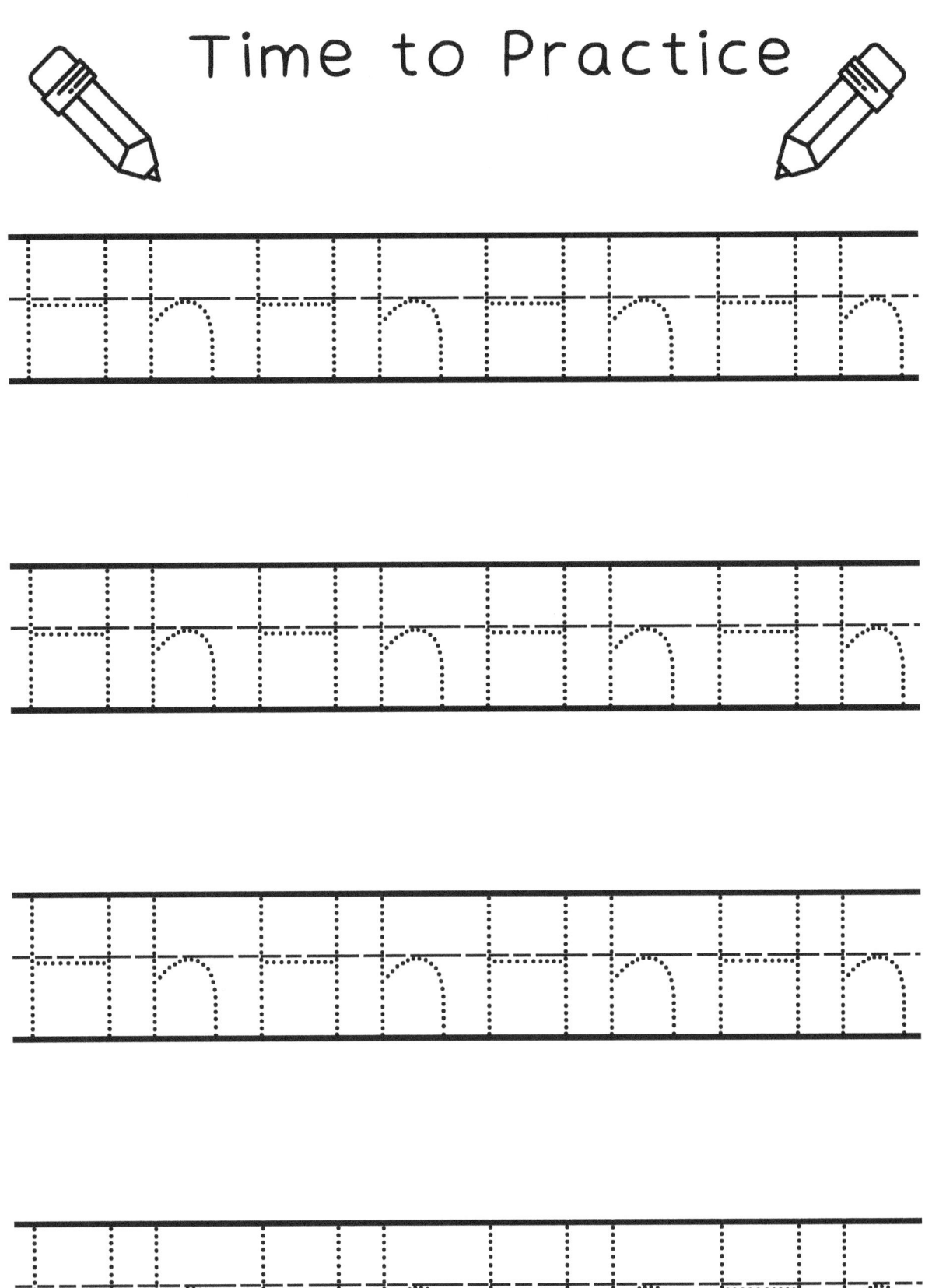

Color Me FUN!

You did it! You traced the hopping 'H.' Ready to color the happy, hopping horse.

H is for Horse

Did you know? Horses are super fast! Some horses can run even faster than a car!

Trace the Icy I

Let's trace the Icy 'I' so Iggy the igloo builder can have an icy door!

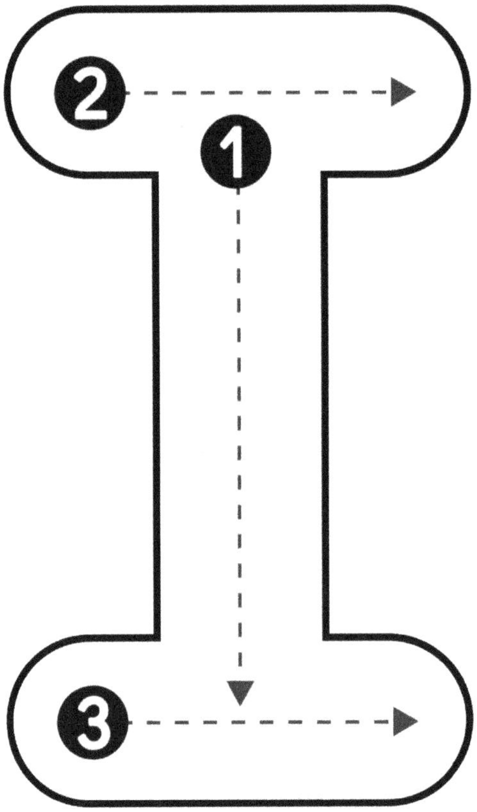

Trace the small alphabet

Let's dip our finger in the <u>i</u>nky dot, and make a tiny 'i' that won't get lost!

Time to Practice

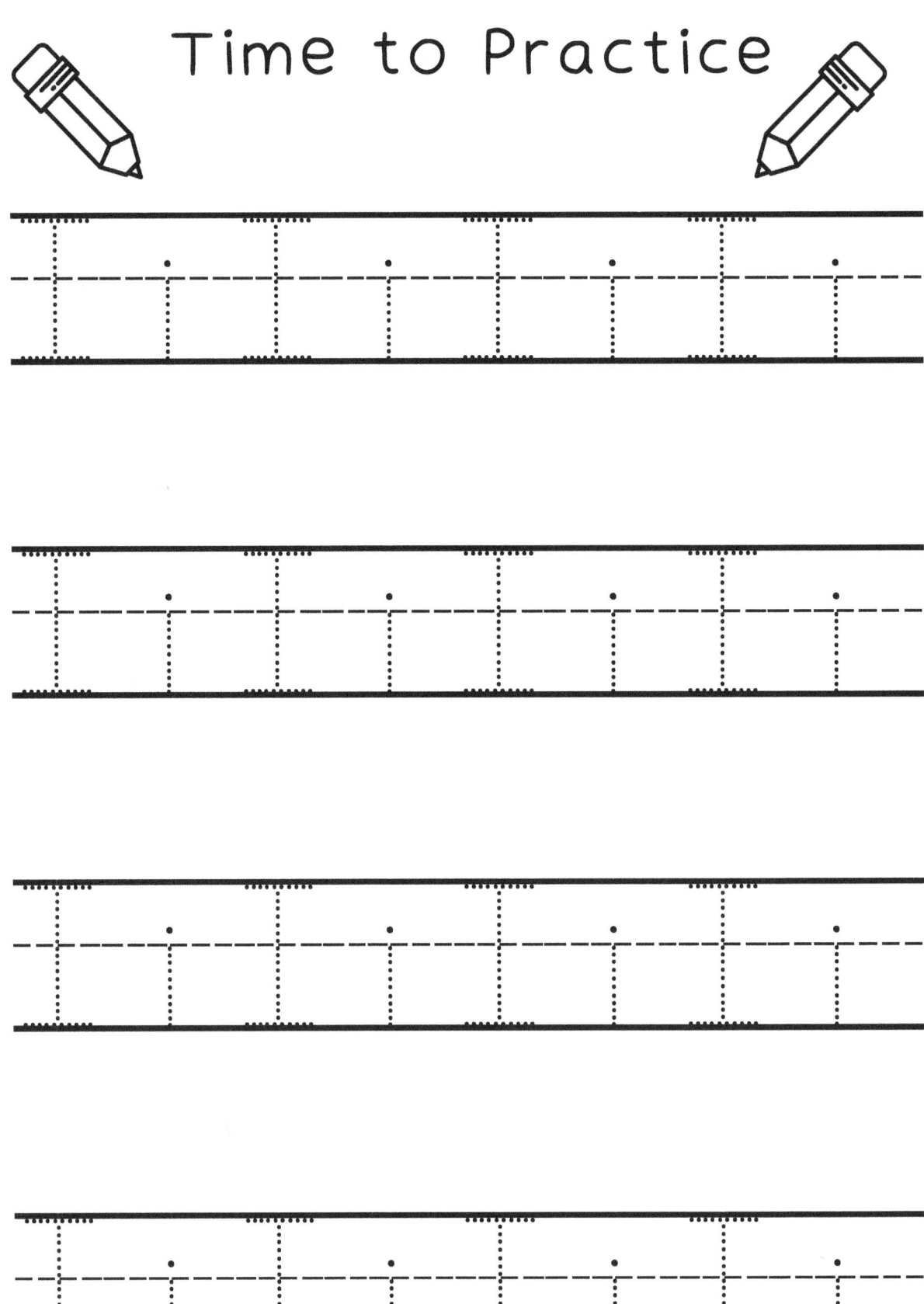

Color Me FUN!

Super job tracing that 'I'! Now let's color Iggy, the iguana. She wants to go to another island to relax under a big palm tree!

I is for Iguana

Did you know? Iguanas have spikey backs. They love to sunbathe and eat leaves.

Trace the Jumping J

The letter 'J' is jumping with joy. Can it jump as high as a happy jellyfish floating in the sea?

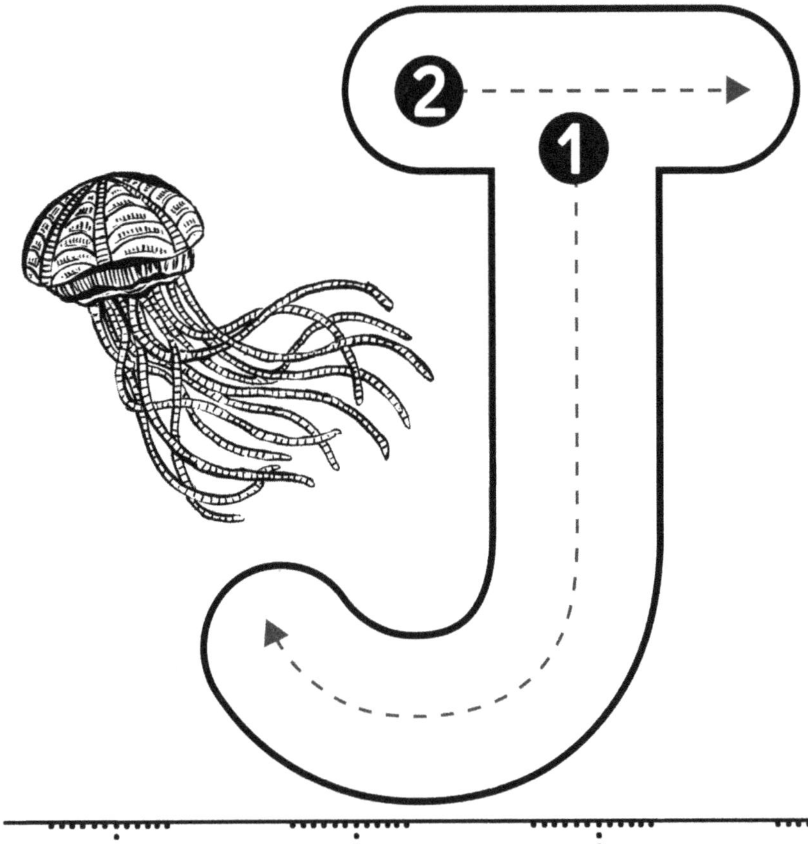

Trace the small alphabet

The jolly 'j' needs some yummy treats! Let's trace it neatly, then give it juice and jam to eat!

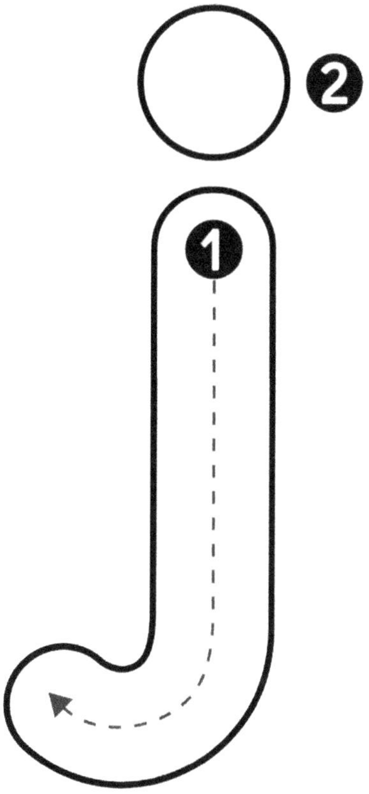

 # Time to Practice

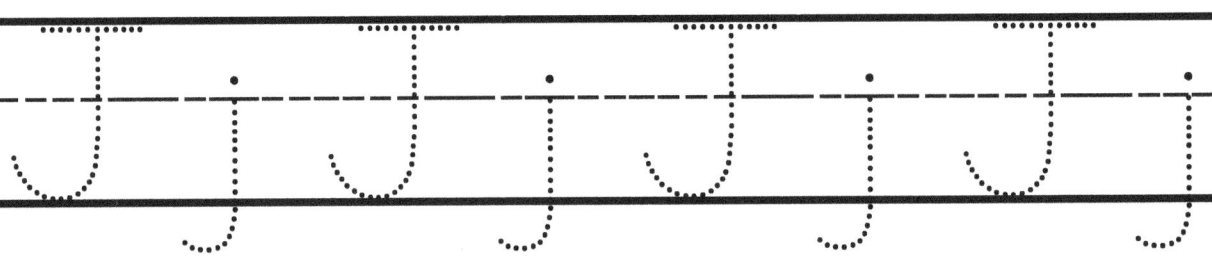

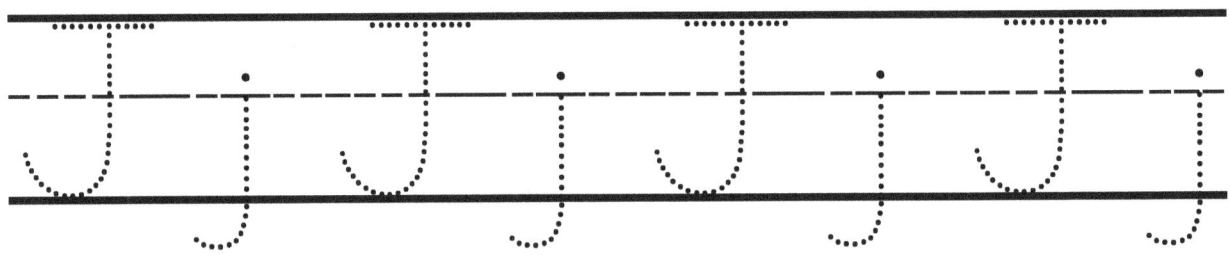

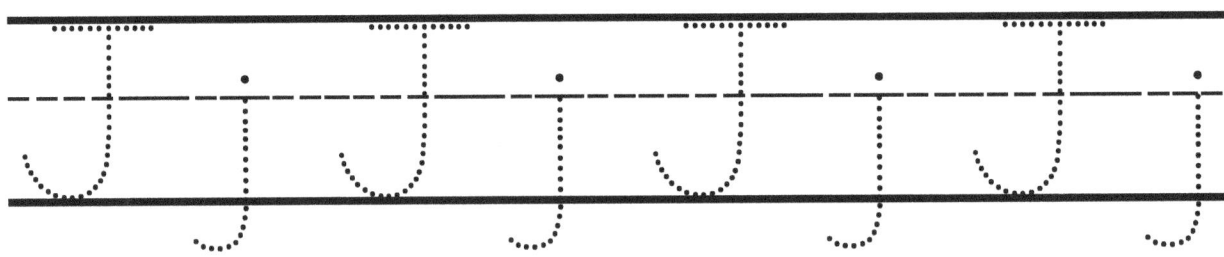

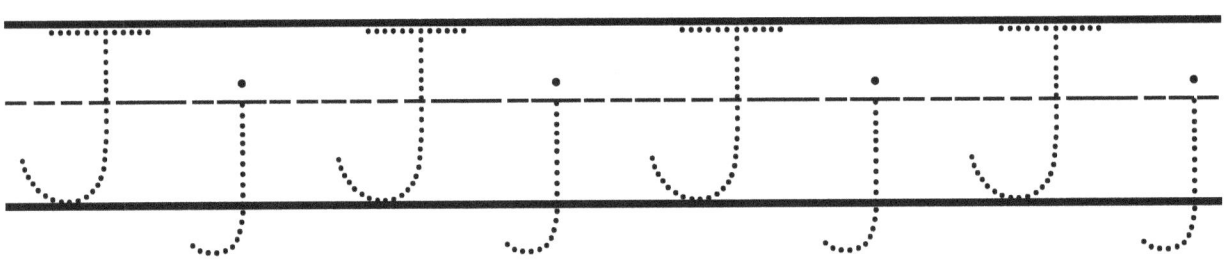

Color Me FUN!

You traced 'J' jolly well. Time to celebrate with Jasper, the joyful Jaguar. Have fun coloring.

J is for Jaguar

Did you know? Jaguars can jump super high, even higher than a house! They use their jumps to catch yummy snacks in the trees!

Trace the King K

The Kangaroo lost its Kite while Kicking its legs high in the air! Let's trace a big 'K' to make a new one.

Trace the small alphabet

Look at that small 'k'! Let's trace it and make it a King!

 # Time to Practice

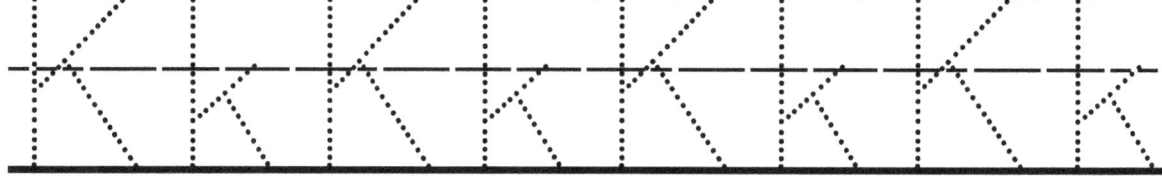

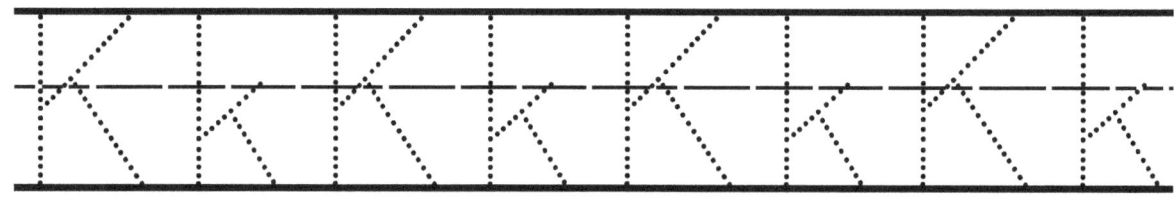

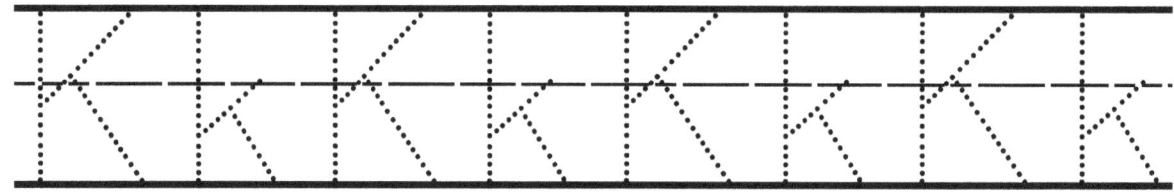

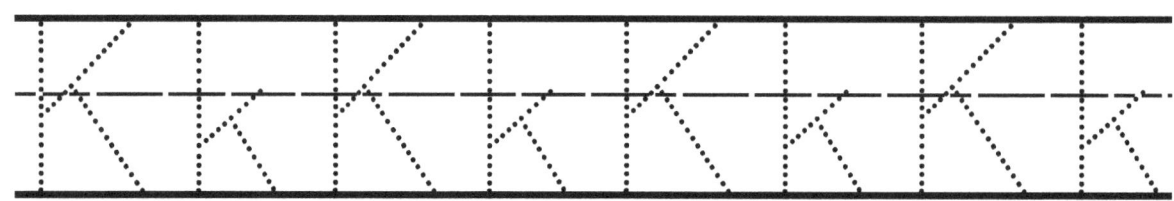

Color Me FUN!

Wow! You traced the King 'K' perfectly. Time to color the Kind Kangaroo!

K is for Kangaroo

Did you know? Kangaroo mamas carry their babies in a special pouch on their tummy!

Trace the Long L

The long 'L' is feeling left out! Let's trace it and find it a friendly lion to play with!

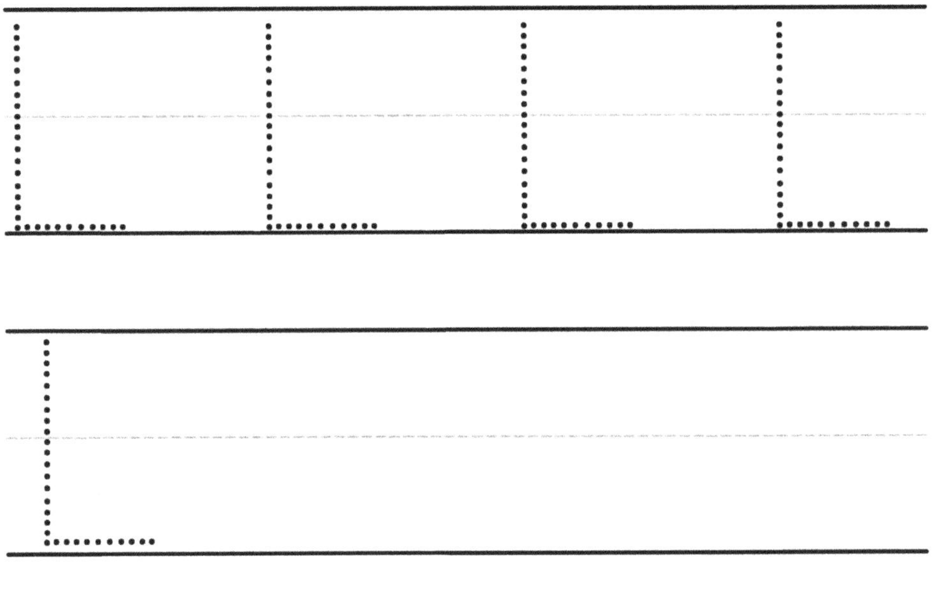

Trace the small alphabet

Look! Luna the ladybug is crawling on a long ladder! Let's trace our small 'l' to help her climb all the way up!

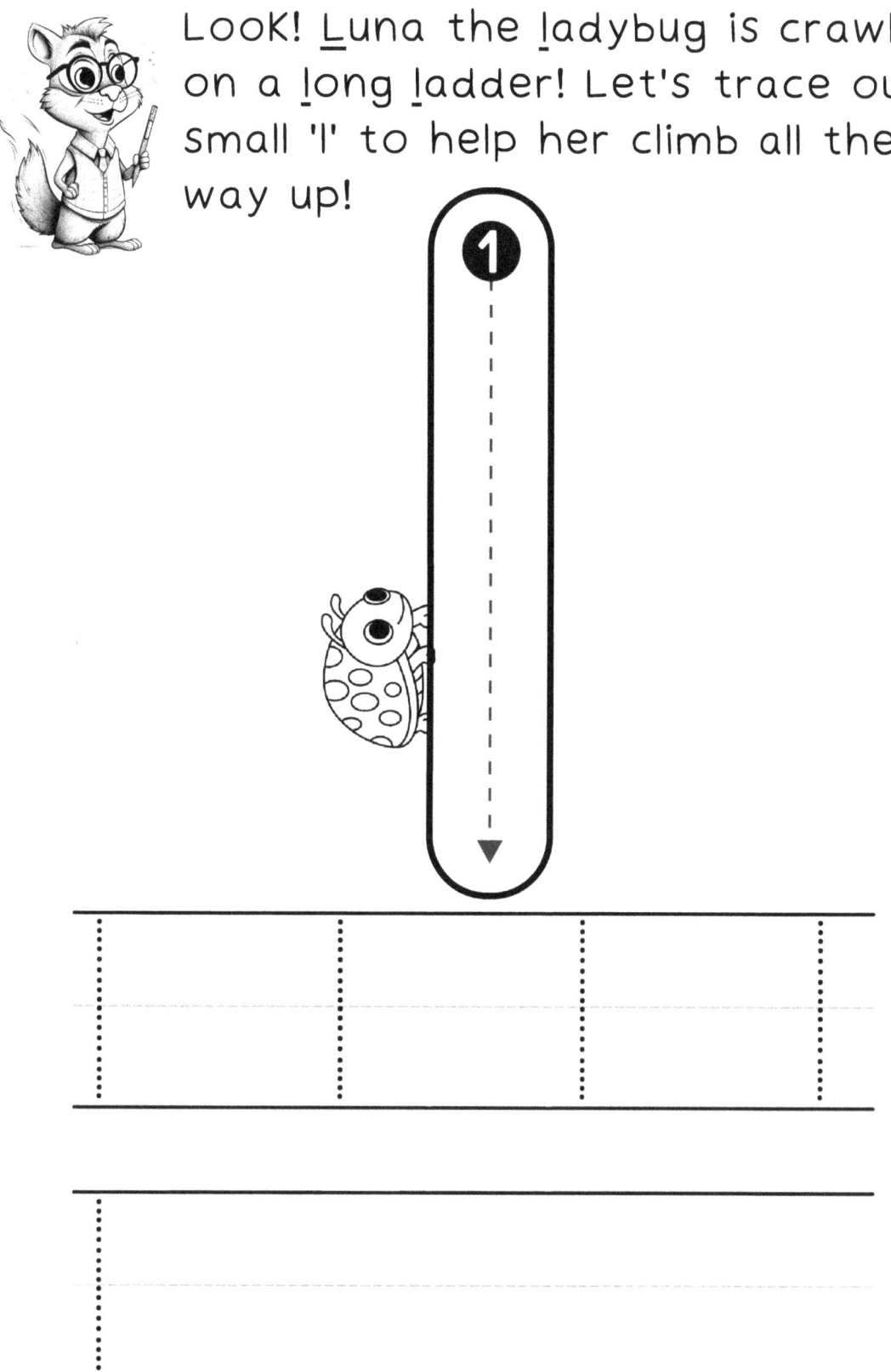

Time to Practice

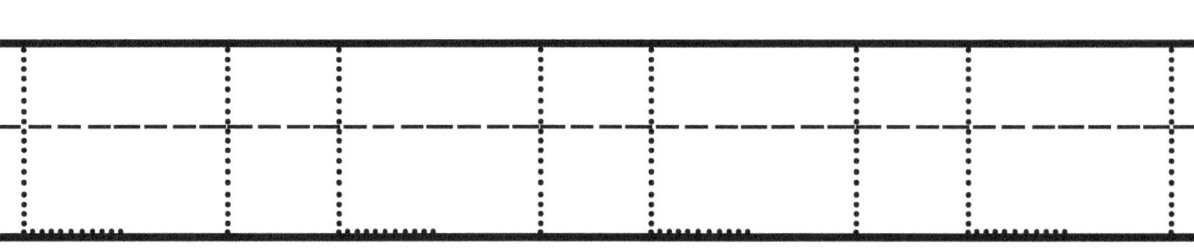

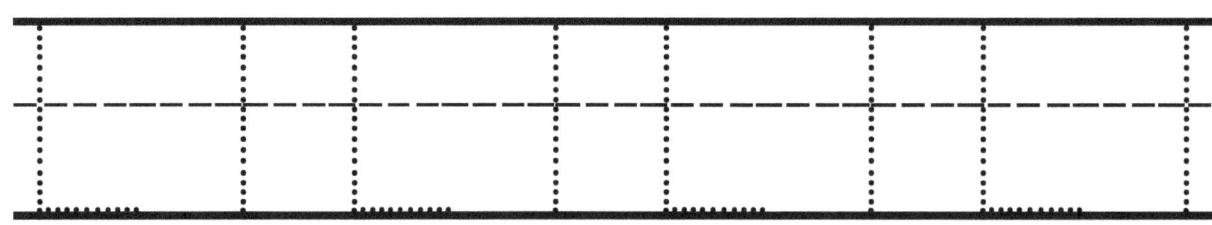

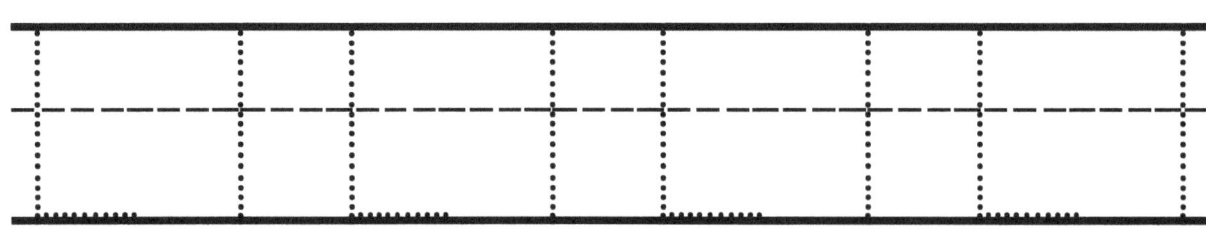

Color Me FUN!

You've traced that 'L' like a pro! Now, let's color the lion. This lion is so lovable. What color mane will you give it?

L is for Lion

Did you know? Lions are the King of the jungle! They have a big, fluffy mane that makes them look extra special.

Trace the Munching M!

Look! The <u>m</u>unching 'M' is having yummy <u>m</u>arshmallows with a cuddly teddy bear on the <u>m</u>oon! Let's trace the 'M' so we can join them!

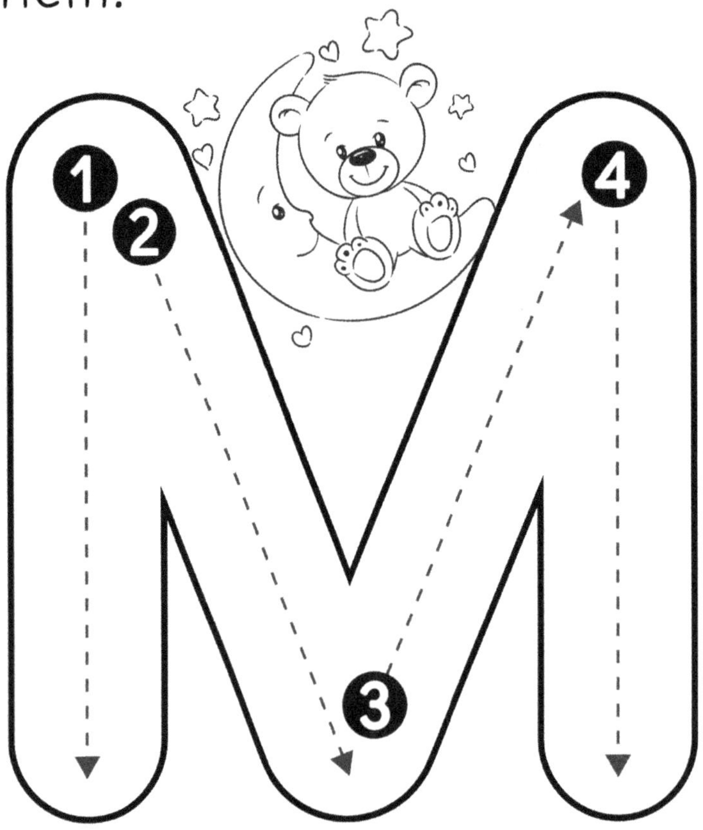

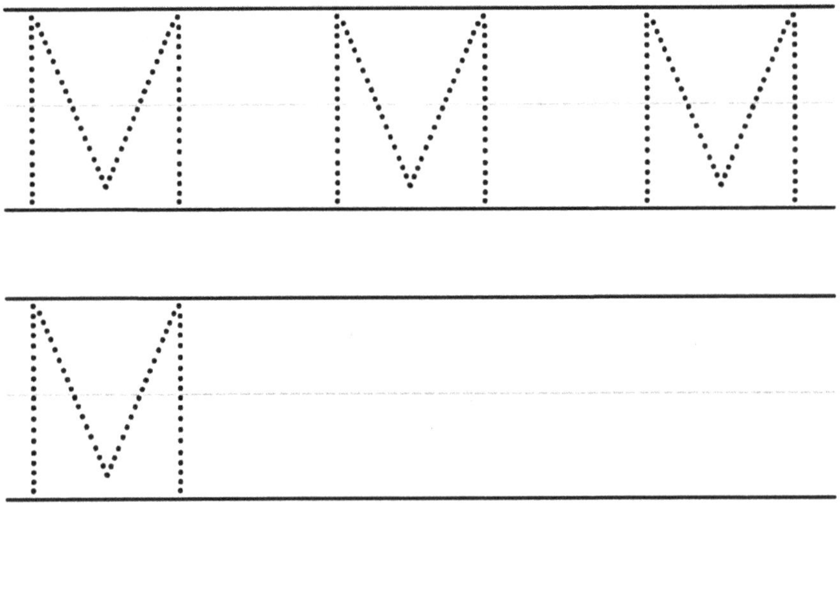

Trace the small alphabet

Wow! That little 'm' reminds me of a friendly <u>m</u>onster's <u>m</u>outh! Let's trace it and see what comes out of it.

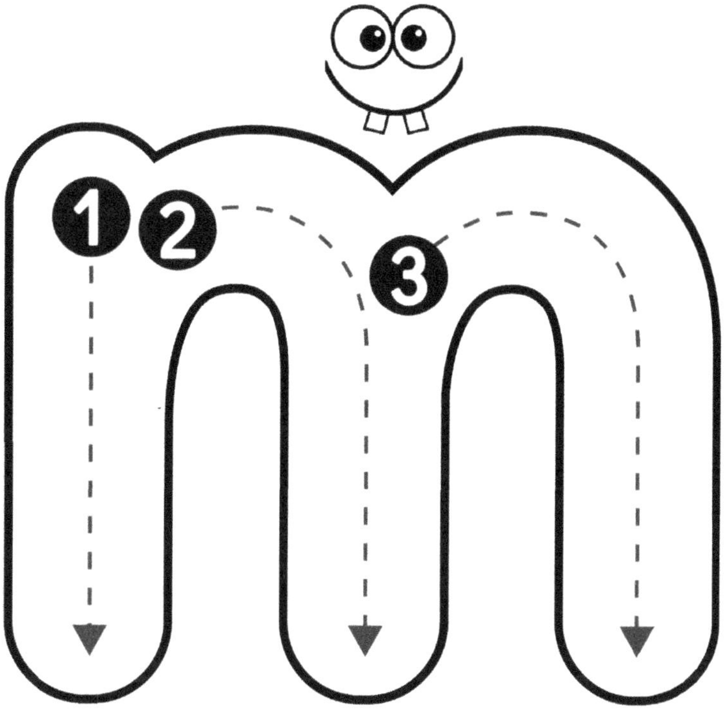

Mushroom

Mango

Time to Practice

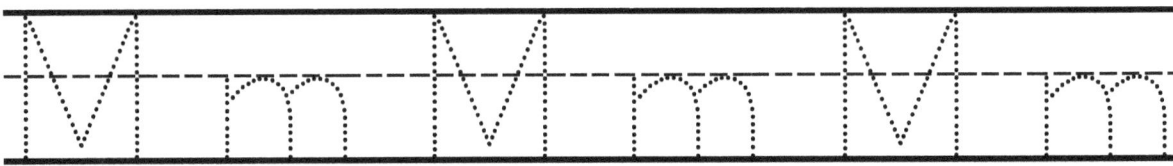

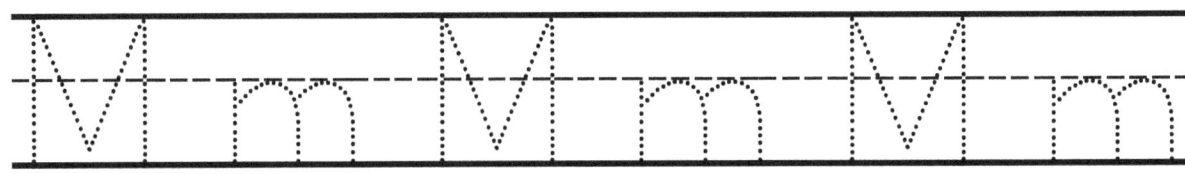

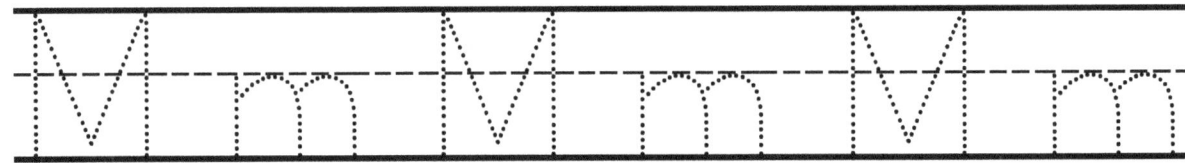

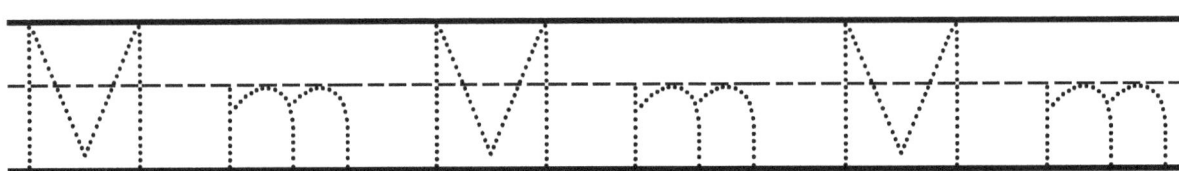

Color Me Fun!

You were <u>m</u>arvelous tracing 'M'! The <u>m</u>onkey is ready for a colorful adventure! Let's color!

M is for Monkey

Did you know? Some monkeys love to eat yummy bananas, but some monkeys also like to eat bugs and leaves!

Trace the N neat!

Look at that big 'N'! It looks like a yummy <u>n</u>oodle soup! Let's trace it <u>n</u>eatly.

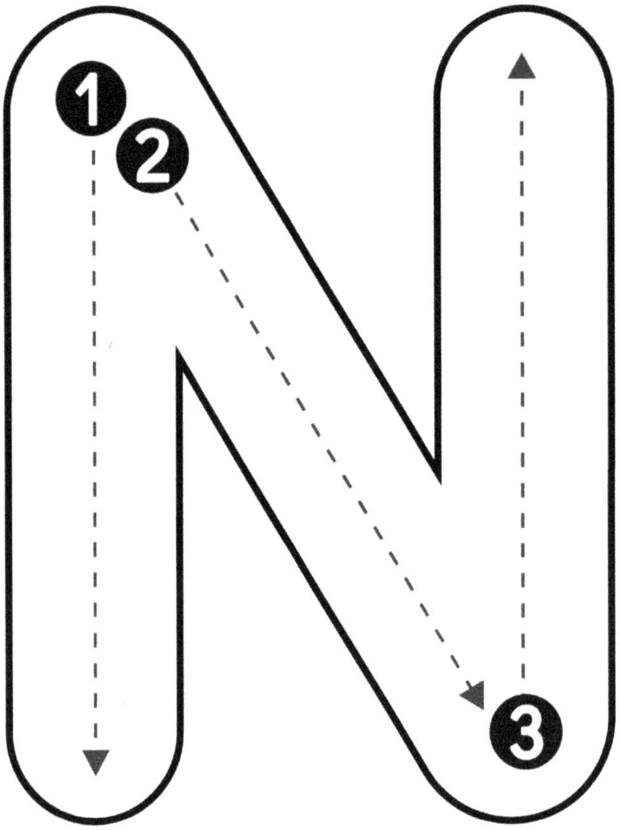

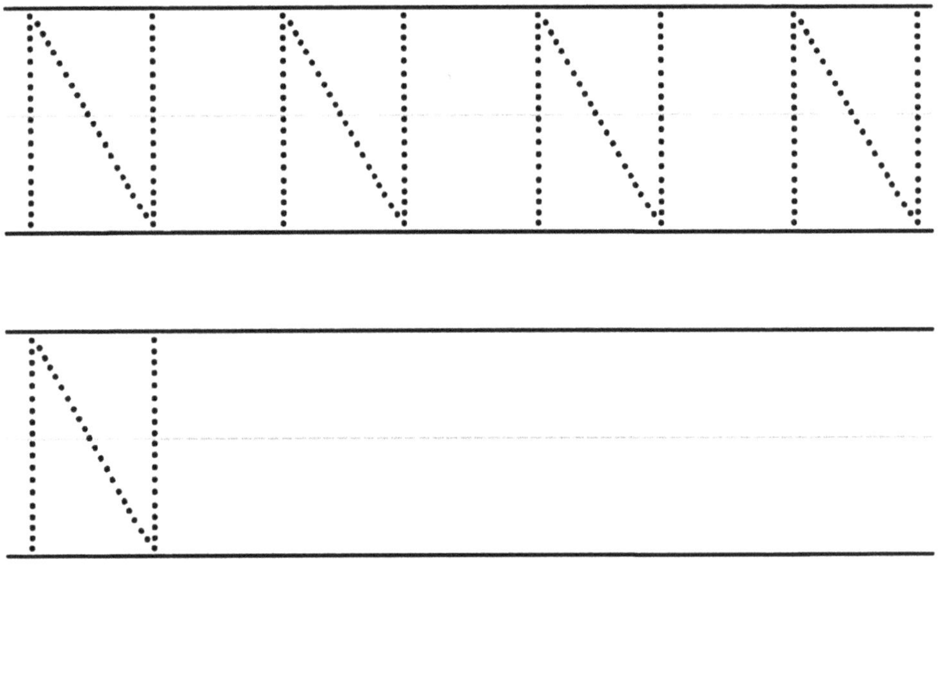

Trace the small alphabet

 The small 'n' is taking a <u>n</u>ap in its <u>n</u>est. Let's quietly trace it so we don't wake it up.

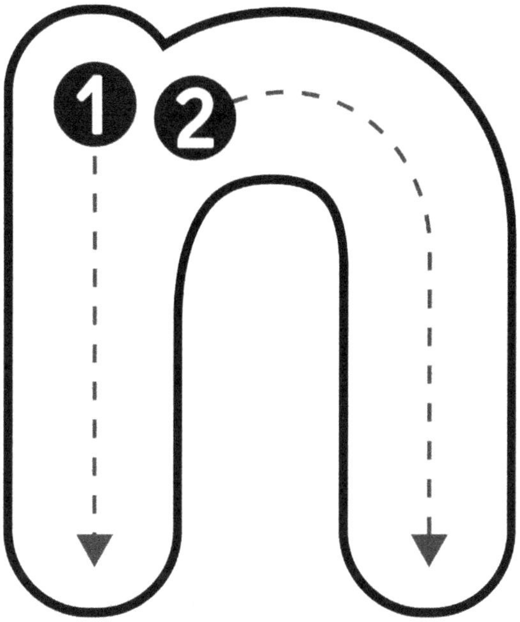

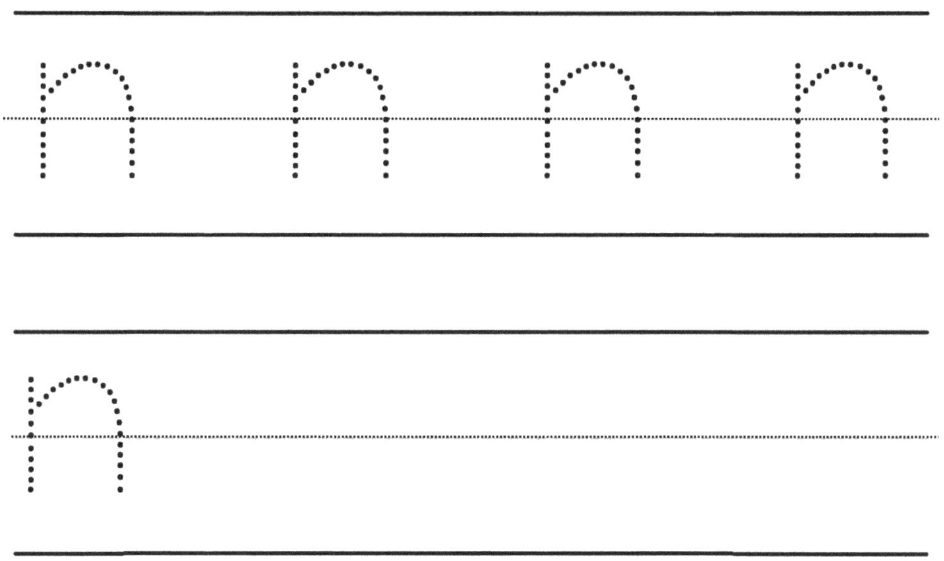

Time to Practice

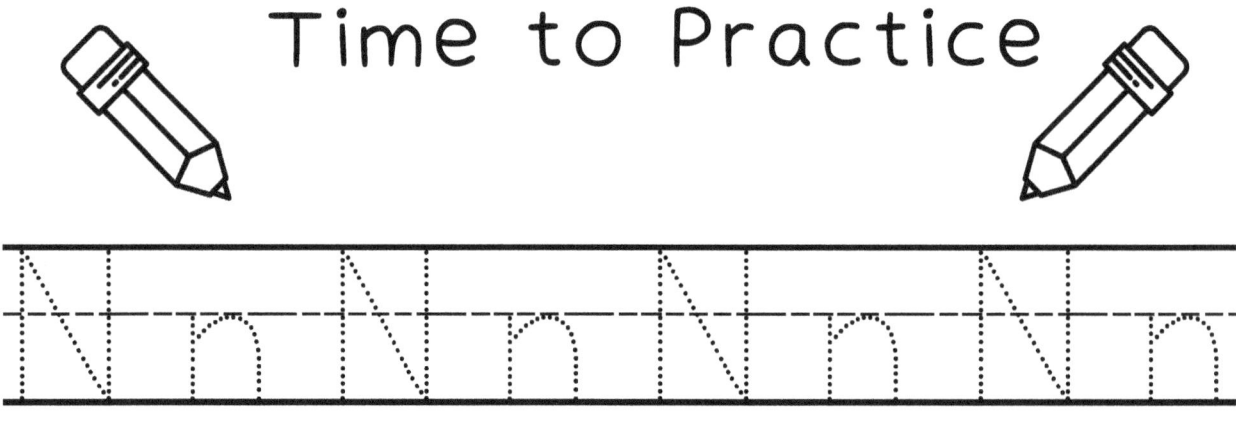

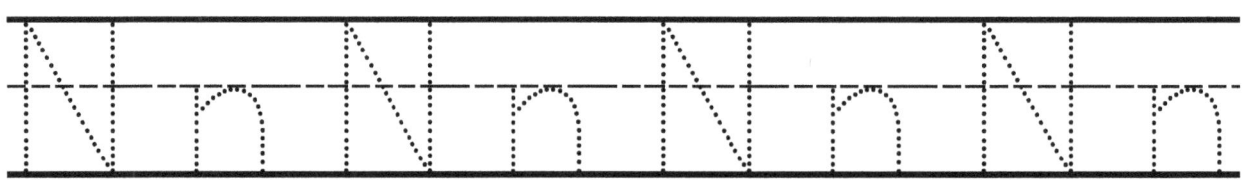

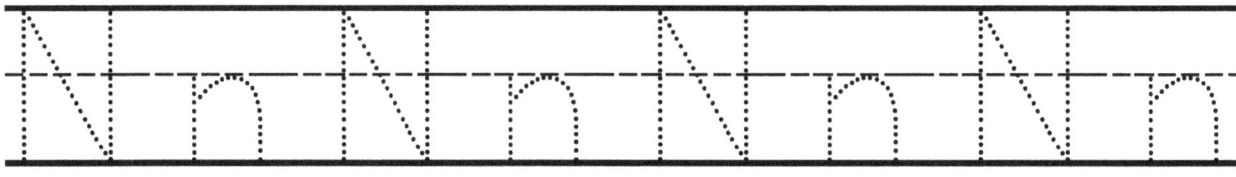

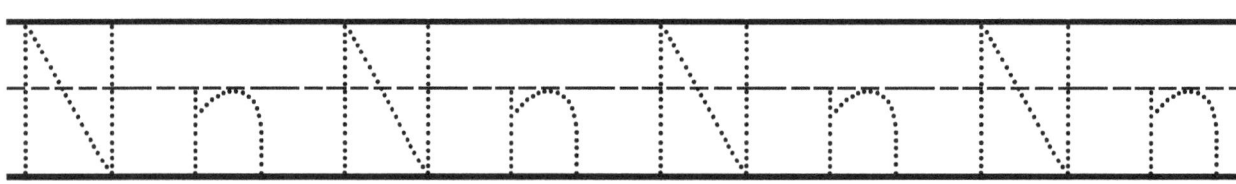

Color Me Fun!

Great tracing! You turned that 'N' into a night sky! Now, let's color a nosy narwhal swimming in the sea along with its neighbor!

N is for Narwhal

Did you know? Narwhals are like unicorns of the sea! They have a long, twisty tusk that comes out of their face!

Trace the Owly O

Wow! The <u>o</u>wl has such big, <u>o</u>utstanding circles for eyes. Let's trace them so it can see all the <u>o</u>wly treats!

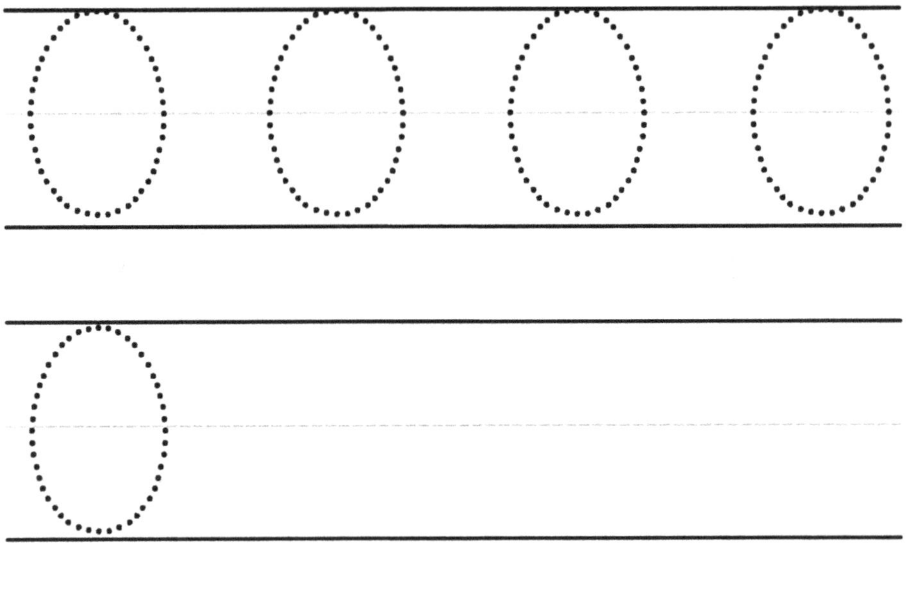

Trace the small alphabet

The small 'o' goes round and round like an <u>o</u>range! Let's trace it and make it juicy!

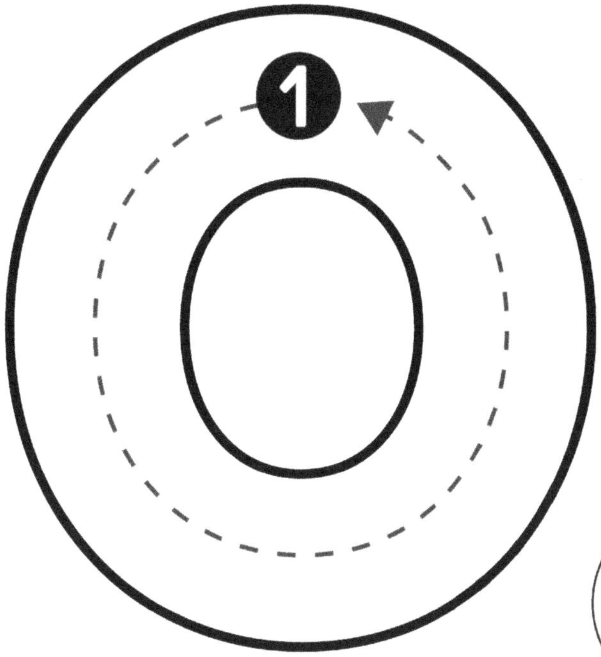

Time to Practice

O o O o O o O o

O o O o O o O o

O o O o O o O o

O o O o O o O o

Color Me Fun!

Wow! Your 'O' shines like a sun! Time to trace a gigantic <u>o</u>ctopus, the biggest <u>o</u>ne in the whole <u>o</u>cean!

O is for Octopus

Did you know? Octopuses have eight long arms. They use them to grab yummy food and play hide-and-seek!

Trace the Playful P

Look at this playful 'P'! Let's trace it so the puppy can find its way to the park!

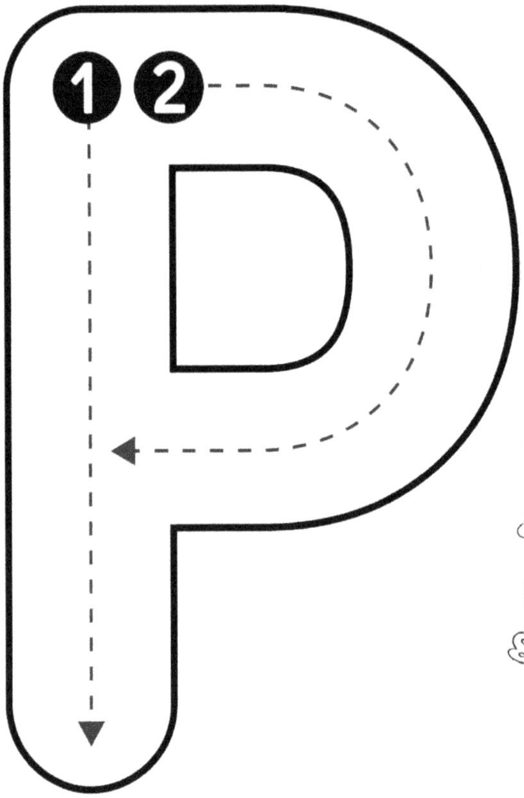

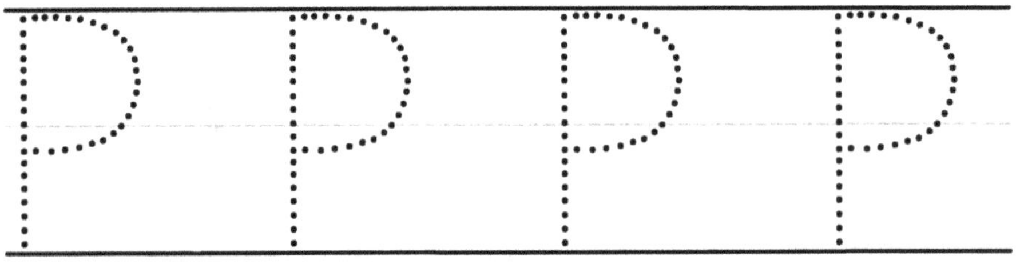

Trace the small alphabet

Have fun tracing the small 'p' like you are playing with a panda.

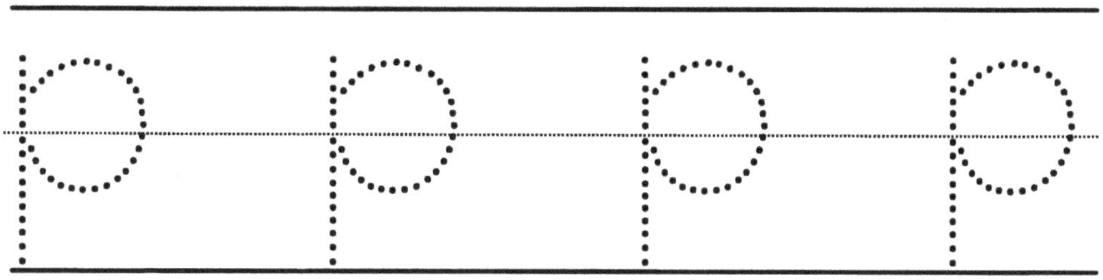

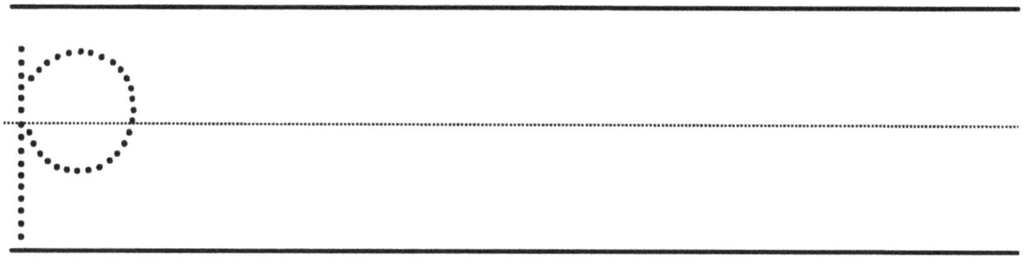

 # Time to Practice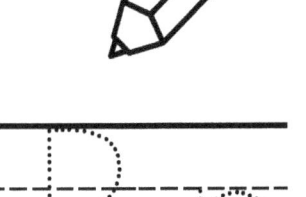

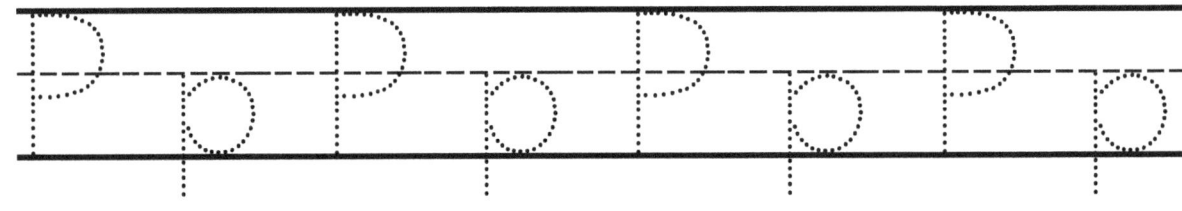

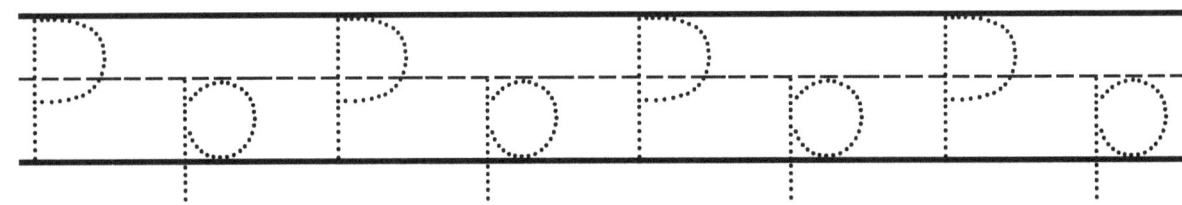

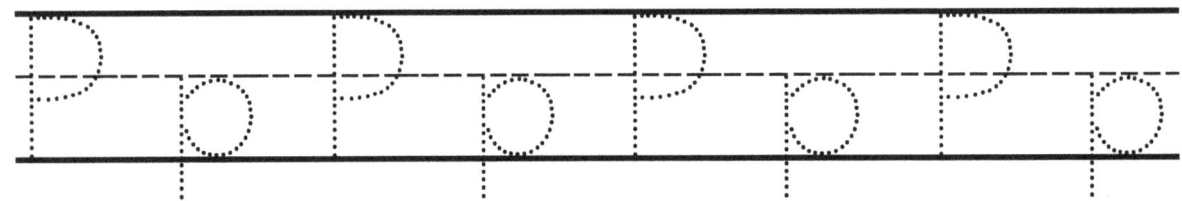

Color Me Fun!

You traced 'P' perfectly. Now let's color this playful penguin and let it waddle on a snowy mountain in Poland!

P is for Penguin

Did you know? Penguins love to slide on their bellies? It's like a super fun snow slide!

Trace the Quacking Q

The 'Q' is practicing its quack! Let's trace the 'Q' and make some silly quacking sounds together!

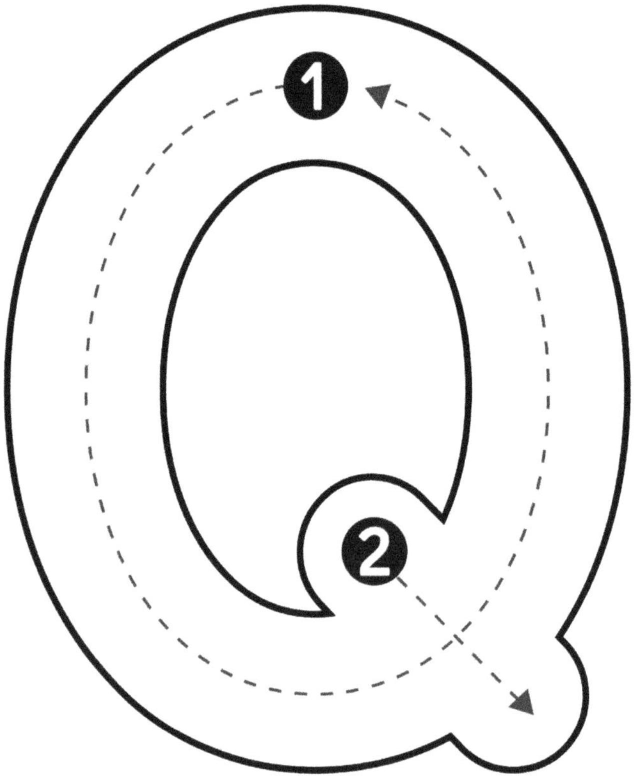

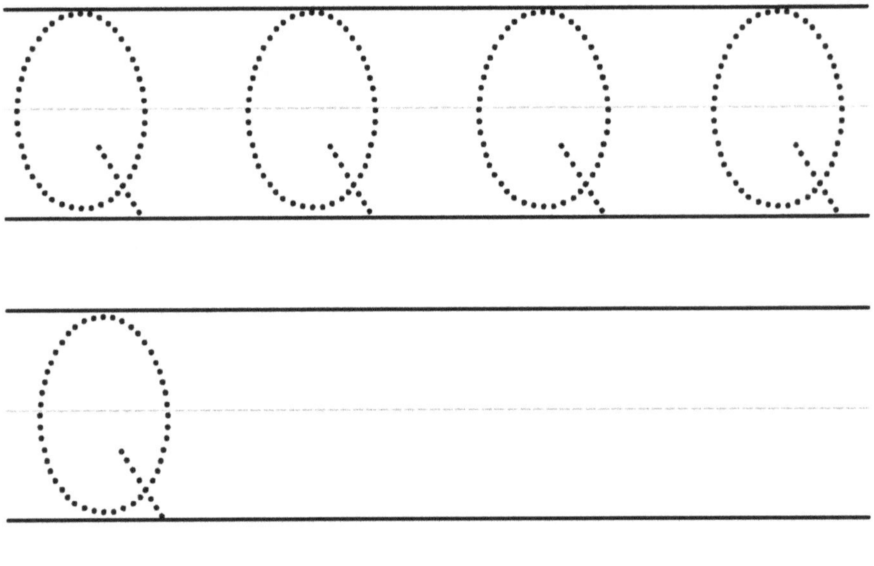

Trace the small alphabet

Let's trace 'q' to see how many funny questions you can come up with?

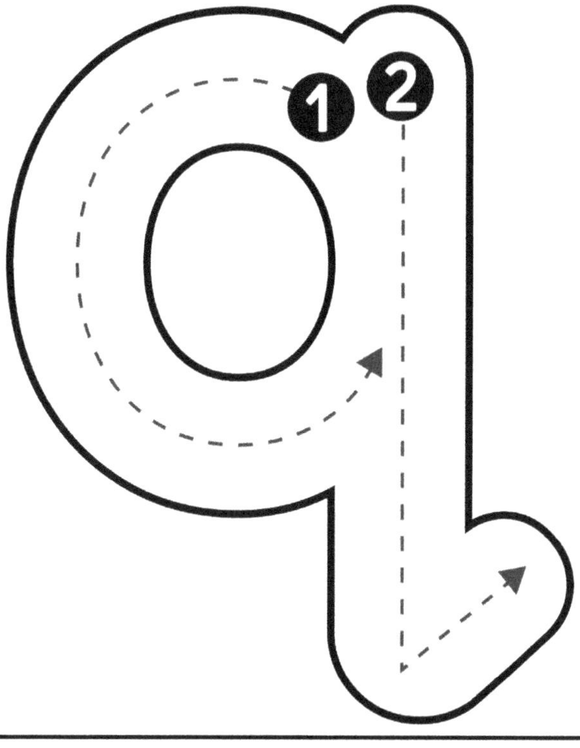

Time to Practice

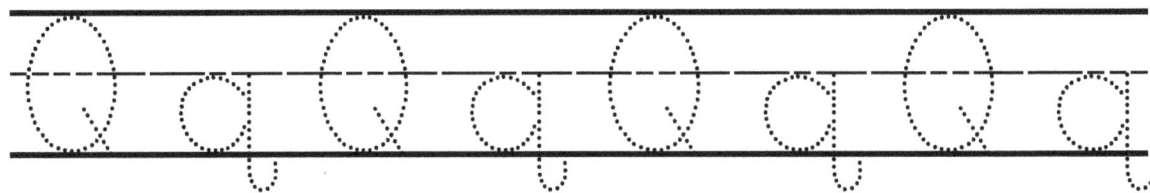

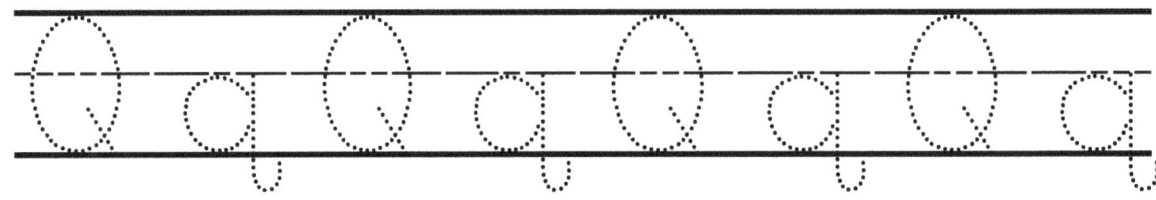

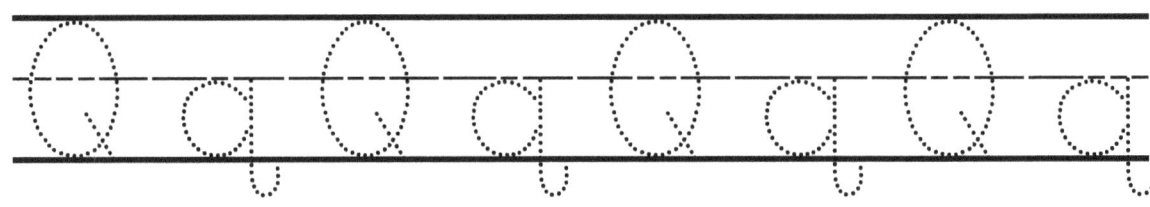

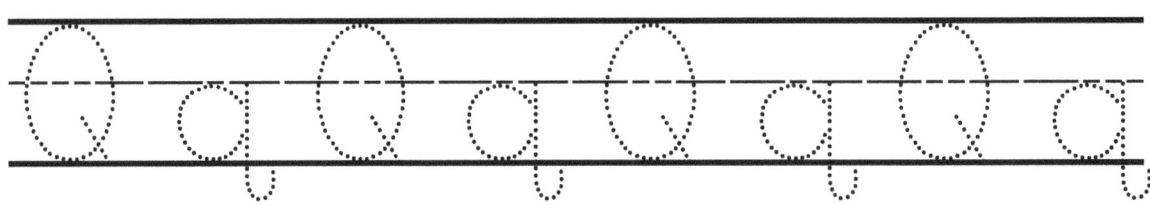

Color Me Fun!

Superstar tracer! The Queen loves your perfect 'Q'! Let's color the Quail and get her ready for the Queen's party!

Q is for Quail

Did you know? Baby quail chicks talk to their mommy quail before hatching by chirping inside their eggs.

Trace the Roaring R

The 'R' is roaring like a lion! Let's trace it and make it the loudest roar ever!

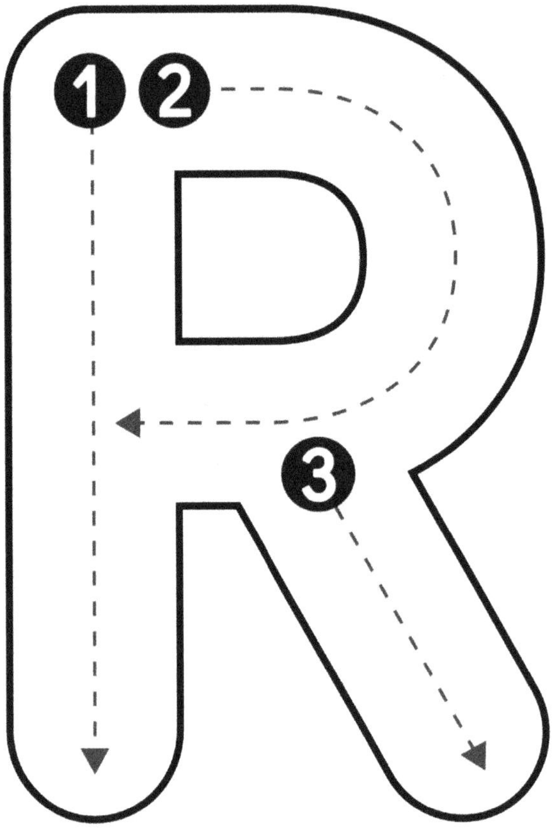

Trace the small alphabet

Look! The small 'r' is the baby <u>r</u>abbit named <u>R</u>ickie. Let's trace it so it doesn't <u>r</u>un away!

Time to Practice

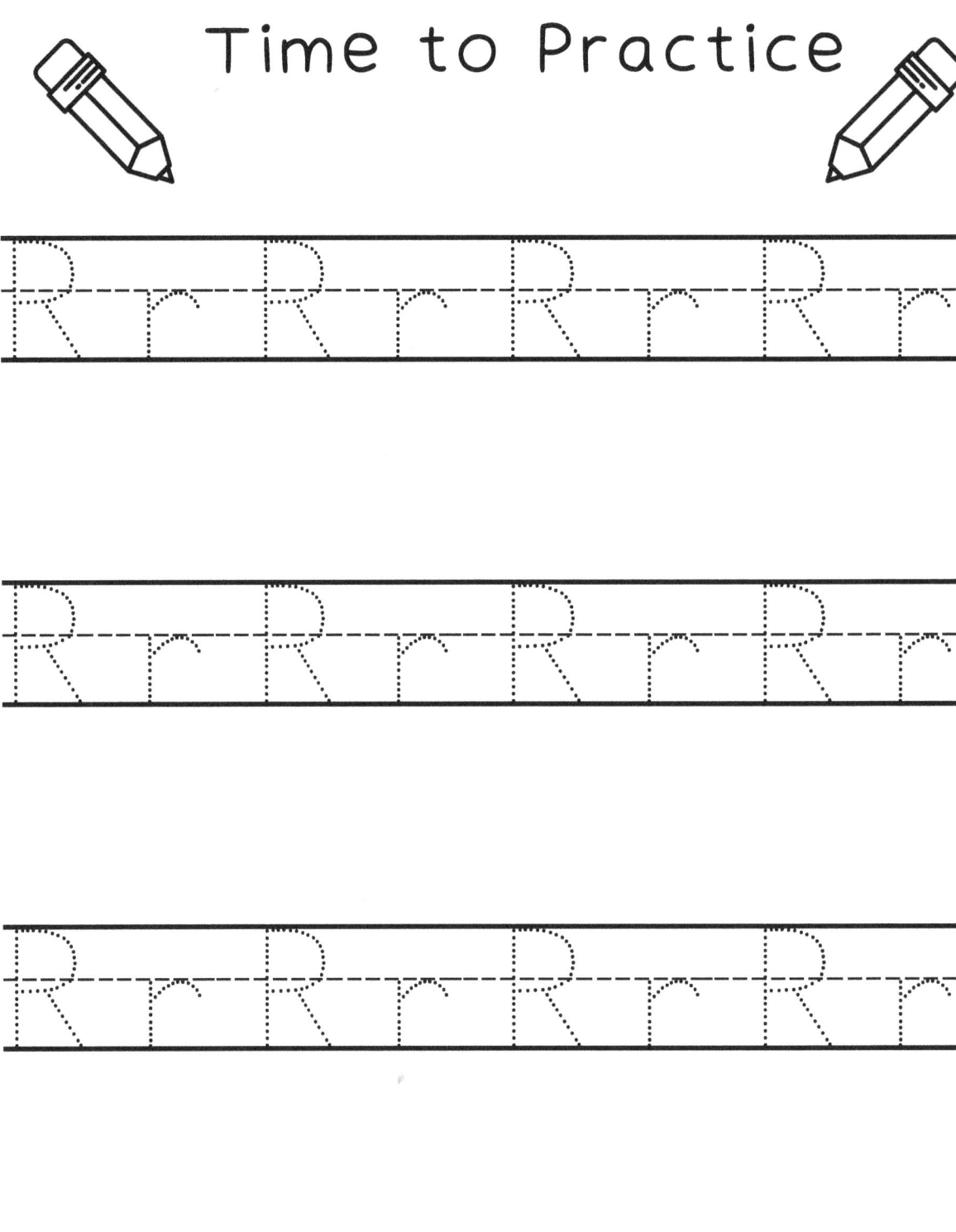

Color Me Fun!

You <u>r</u>ocked tracing 'R'. <u>R</u>eady for some <u>r</u>eindeer color fun!

R is for Reindeer

Did you know? Reindeer noses are super cool! They can turn bright red in the cold weather to help them breathe better.

Trace the Silly, Sneaky S

 Look! The silly 'S' wants to be a surprise! Maybe a strawberry or a swan? Let's trace it and see what it turns into!

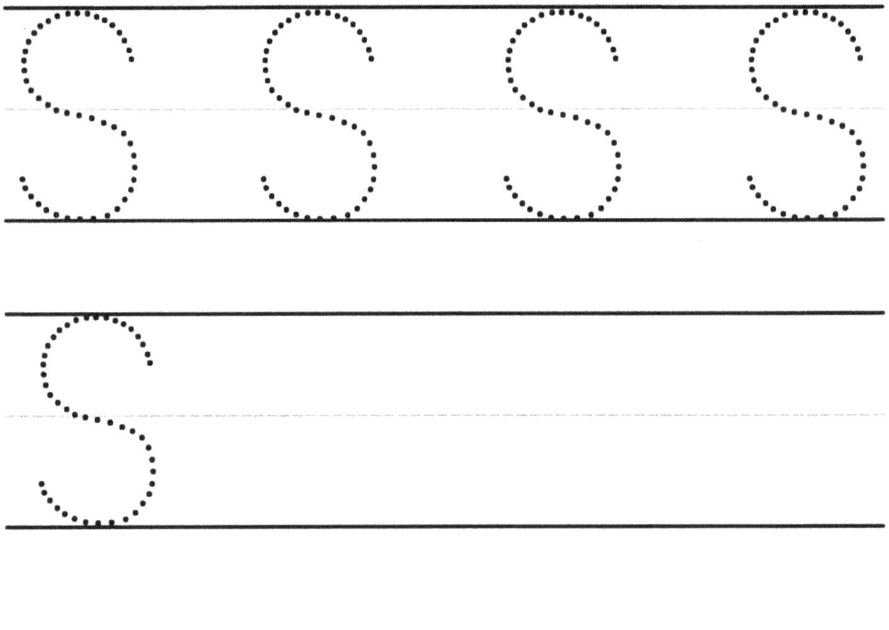

Trace the small alphabet

<u>S</u>hh! The <u>s</u>neaky little 's' is hiding in the corner! Let's trace it <u>s</u>low and see if it turns into a <u>s</u>quishy <u>s</u>nail or <u>s</u>parkly <u>s</u>tars!

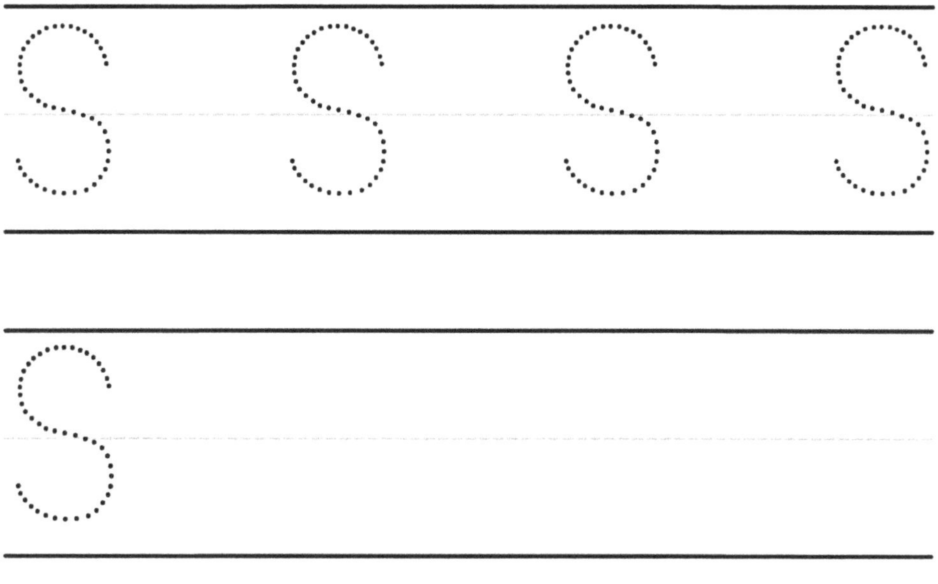

Time to Practice

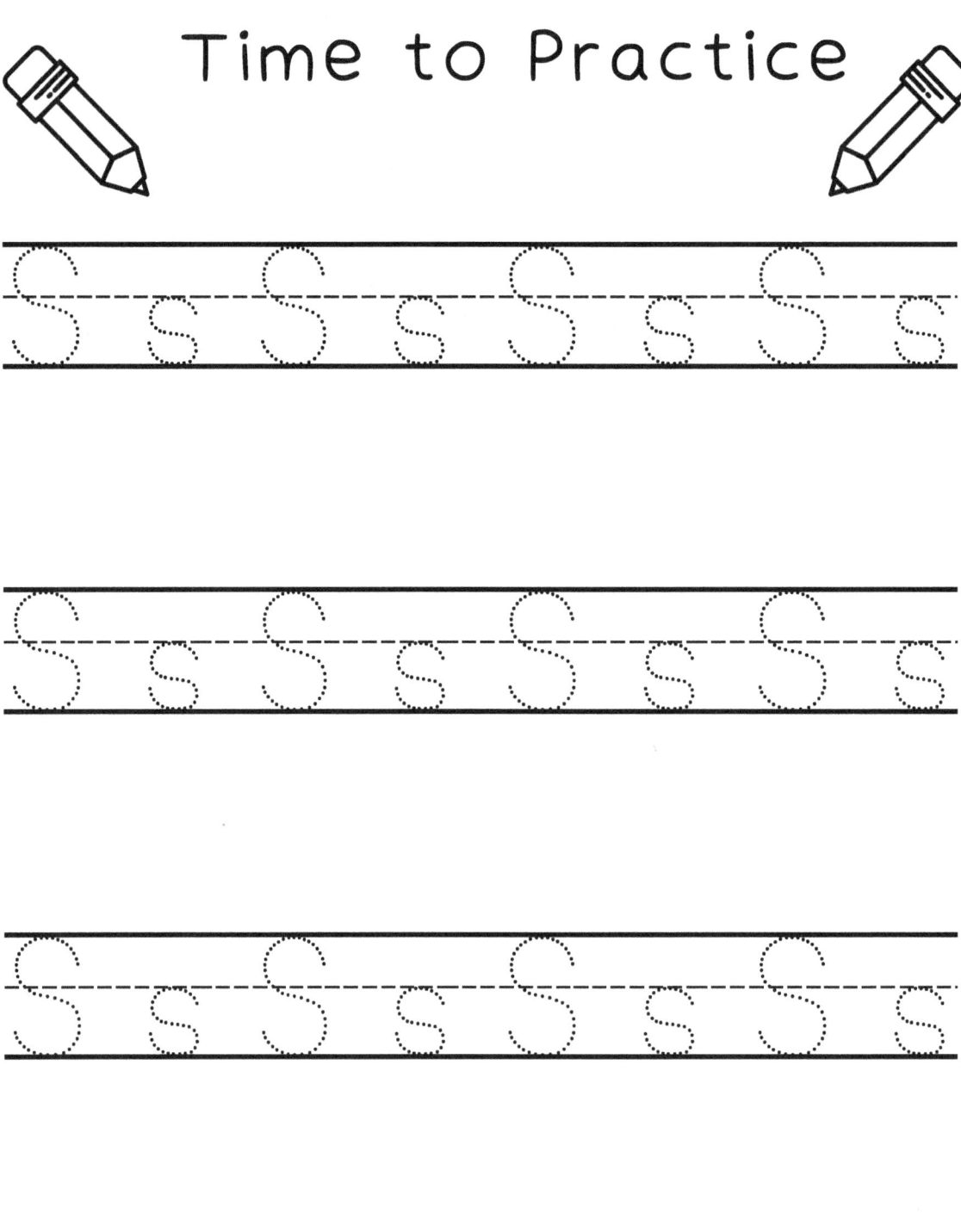

Color Me Fun!

You are a <u>s</u>uperstar tracer! Now, let's color the <u>s</u>quirrel and its long and curly tail. It's the <u>s</u>illiest, <u>s</u>quiggliest tail ever!

S is for Squirrel

Did you know? Squirrels can climb trees faster than you can run! They have sharp claws that help them grip the bark.

Trace the Tall T

Look! A tall 'T' needs our help! Let's trace it and watch it turn into a tree.

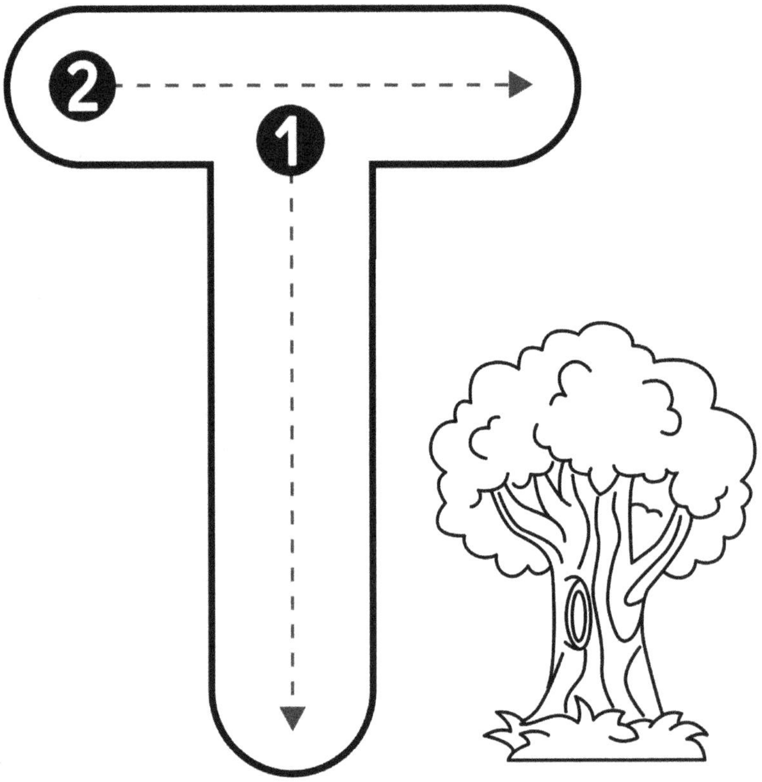

Trace the small alphabet

Time to be a tiny train! Let's trace along the lines of the small 't' and see where it goes!

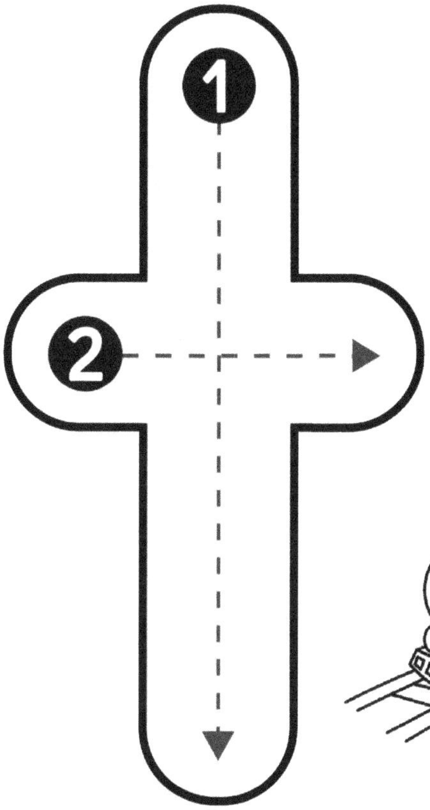

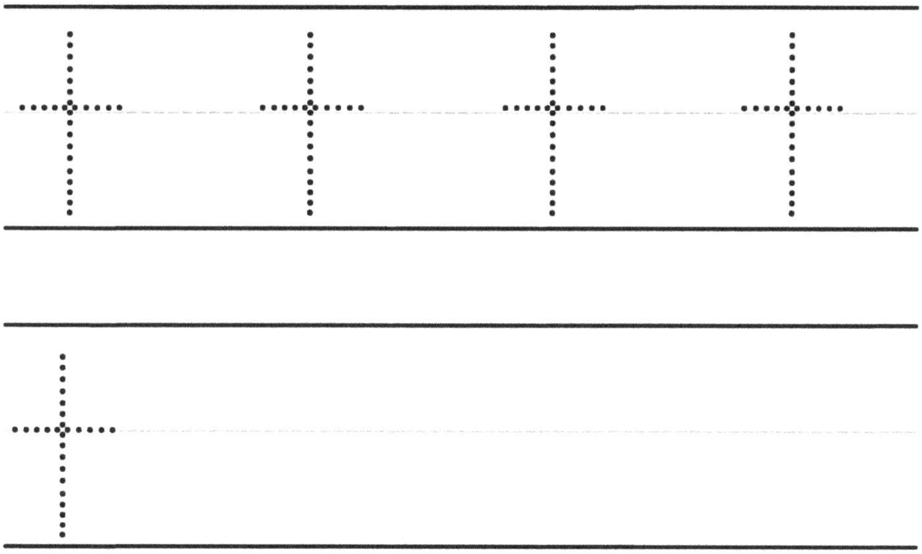

Time to Practice

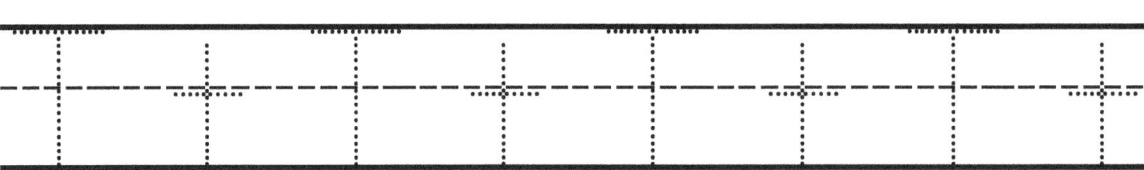

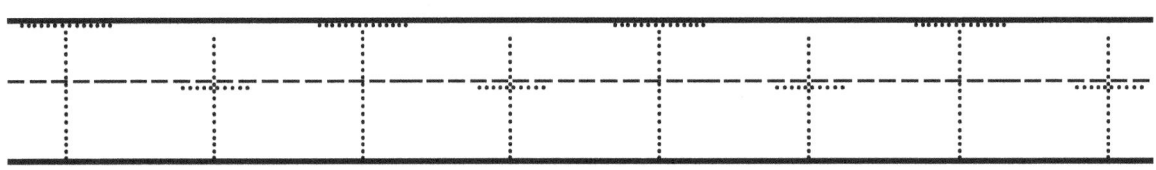

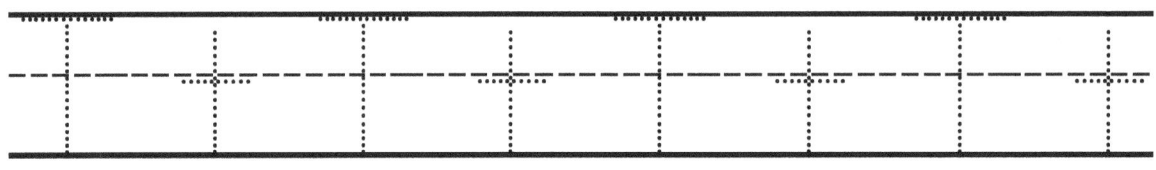

Color Me Fun!

You are a <u>t</u>alented <u>t</u>racer! Ready to color <u>T</u>ony, <u>t</u>he <u>t</u>urtle. He loves swimming in warm water. Can you draw some waves around it?

T is for Turtle

Did you Know? Turtle shell protects them from bumps and Keeps them safe.

Trace the U up

Let's trace the 'U' up high! See what kind of an upside down silly face it makes. Wow! That's a super silly face!

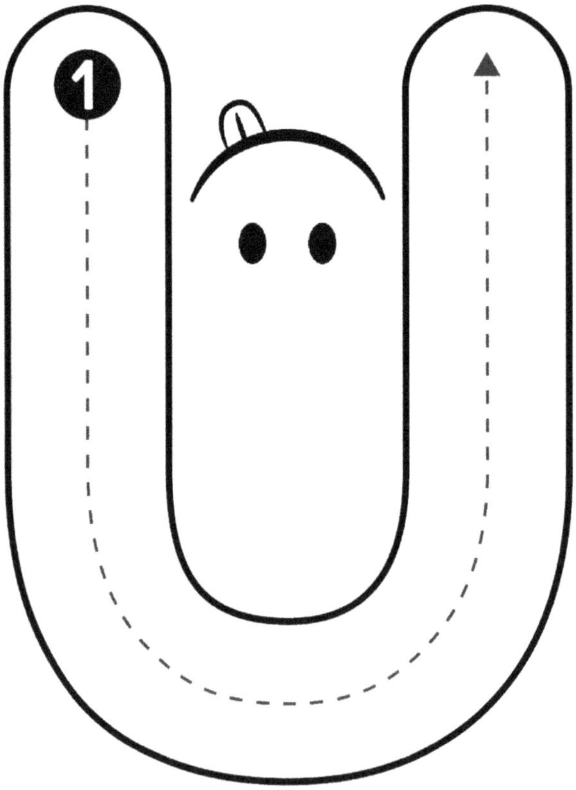

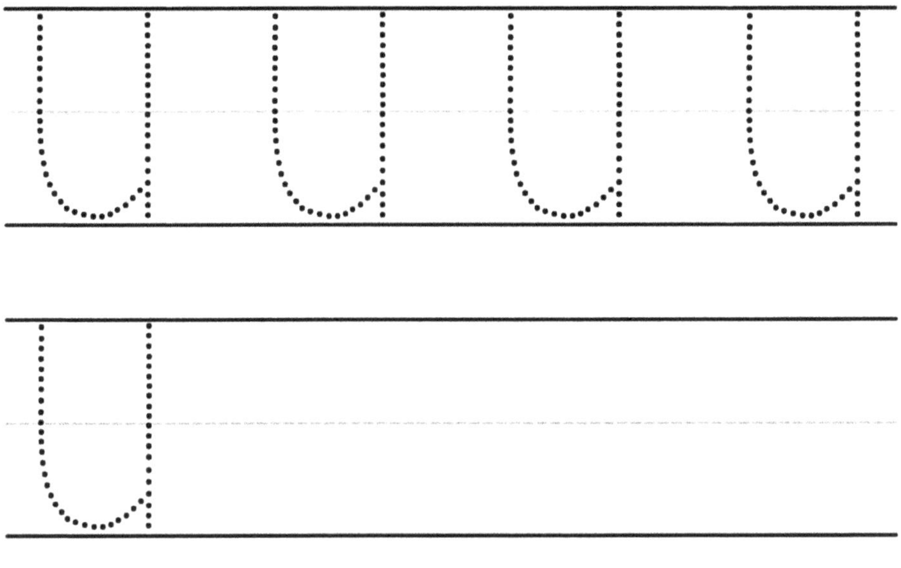

Trace the small alphabet

Uh oh! The small 'u' is lost in the rain! Let's follow its <u>u</u>mbrella and see where it goes again!

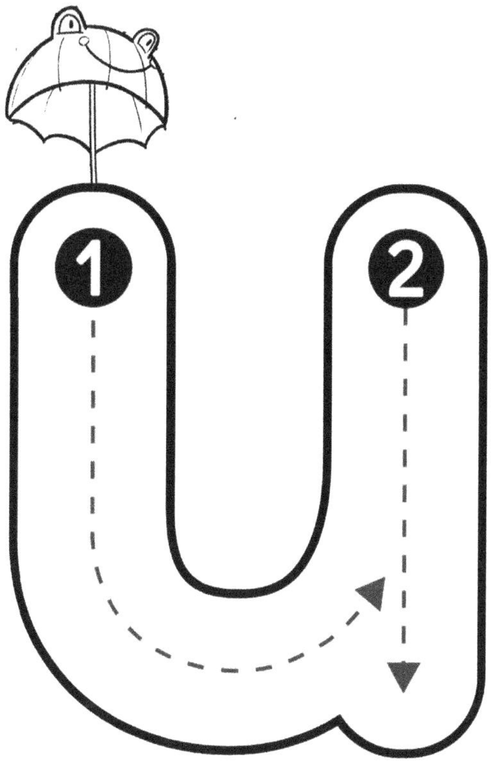

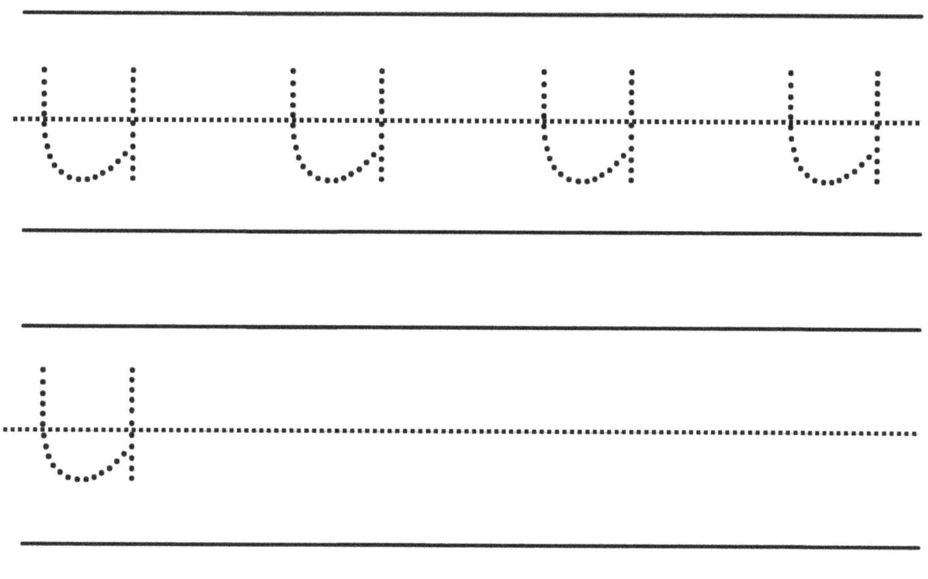

Time to Practice

Color Me Fun!

You are an <u>u</u>ltimate tracer! Time to grab your favorite colors and make that <u>u</u>nicorn sparkle!"

U is for Unicorn

Did you know? Unicorns are special horse-like creatures in stories and fairytales! People love to imagine them with sparkly horns and magical powers!

Trace the Victory V

Look at that big 'V'! Let's trace it to sing a happy <u>v</u>ictory song!

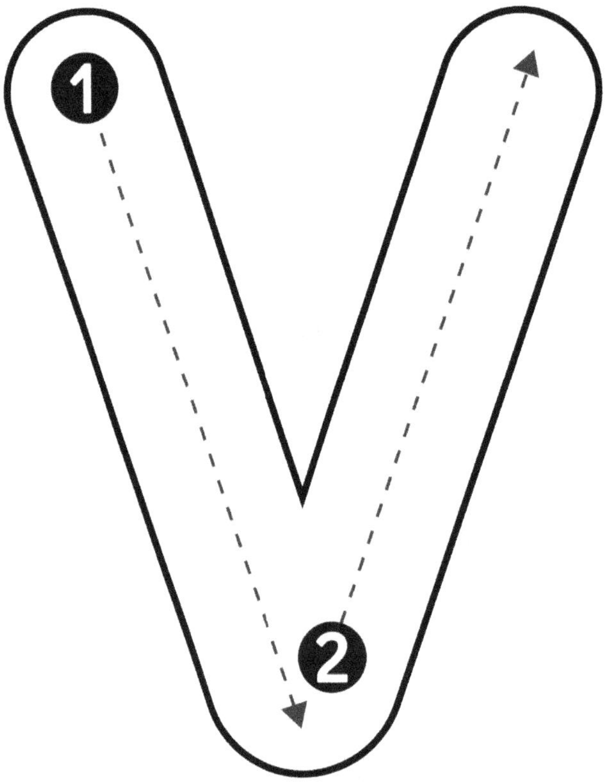

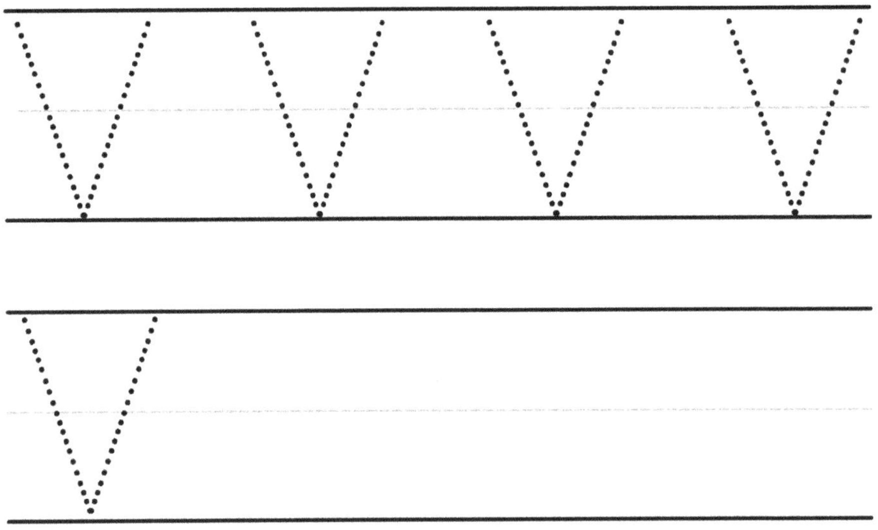

Trace the small alphabet

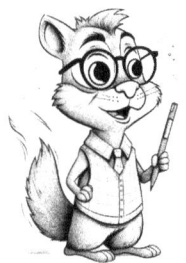

LooK, the yummy vegetables are riding on the van to go to a veggie party. Let's trace the small 'v' so they are not late for the party.

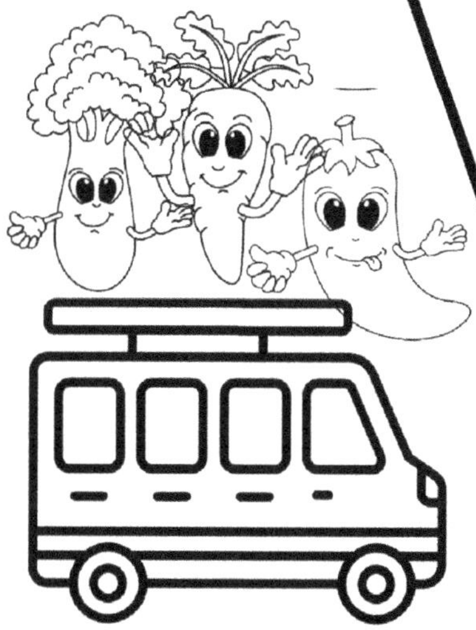

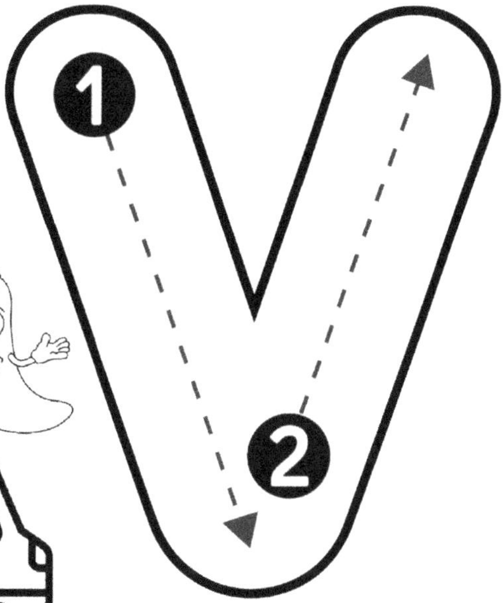

v v v v

v

Time to Practice

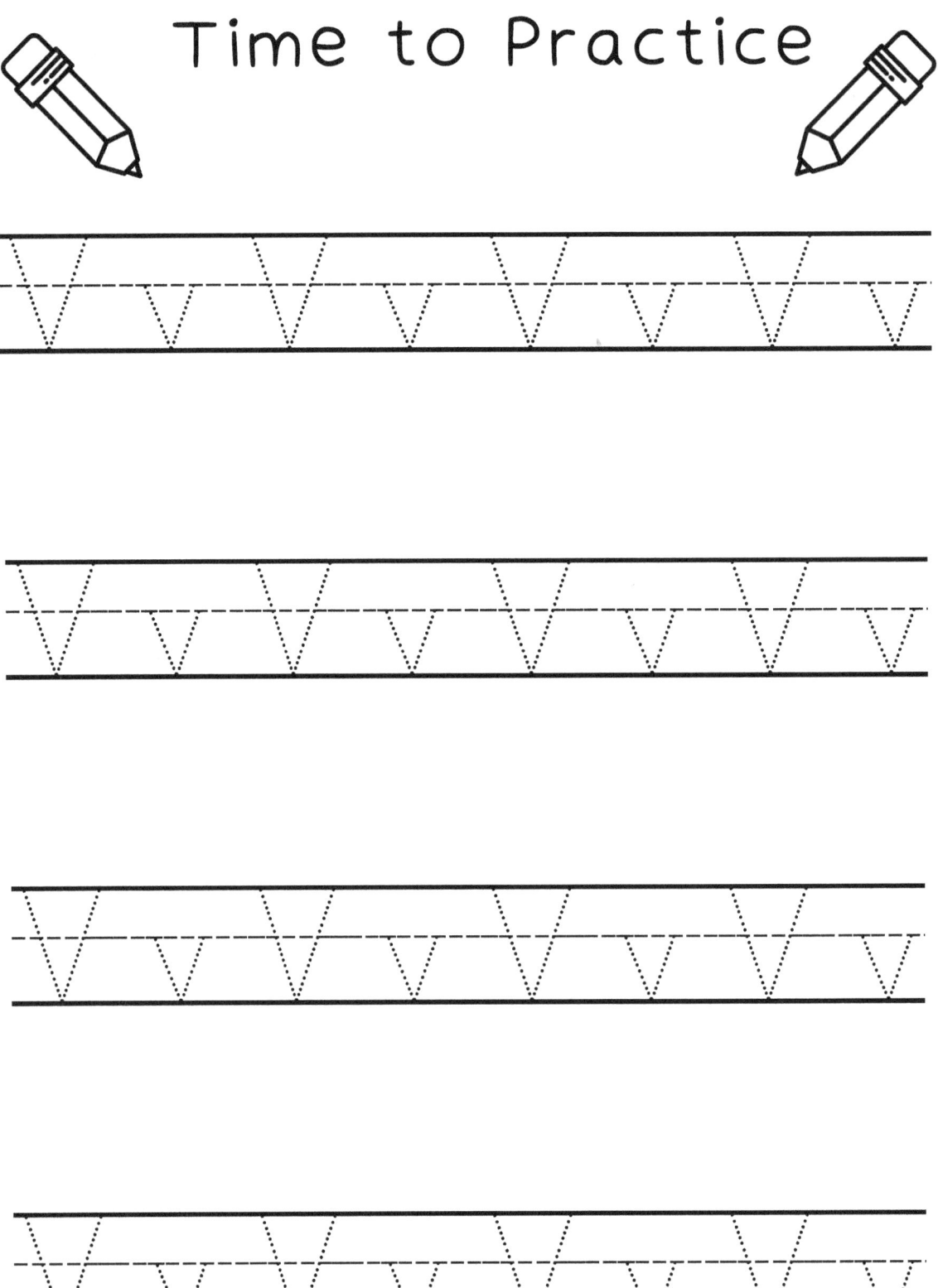

Color Me Fun!

You were superb tracing the 'V'! Now let's get colorful and make that <u>v</u>ulture happy!

V is for Vulture

Did you know? Vultures have big, bald heads and they like to hang out on high rocks.

Trace the Wiggly W

Trace the 'W', up and down! Maybe a silly <u>w</u>orm will <u>w</u>iggle out its nose!

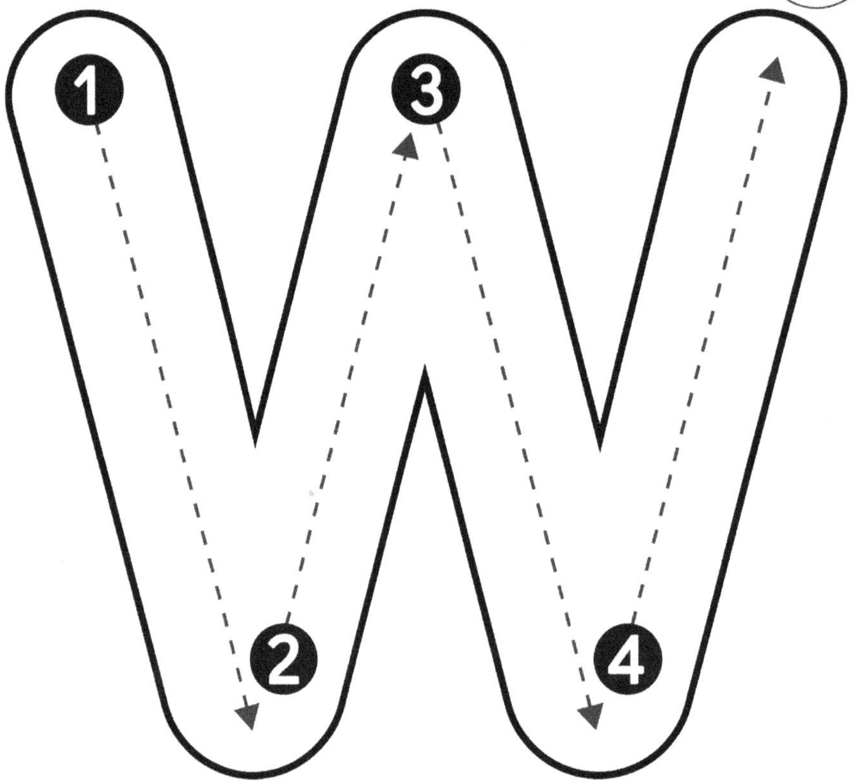

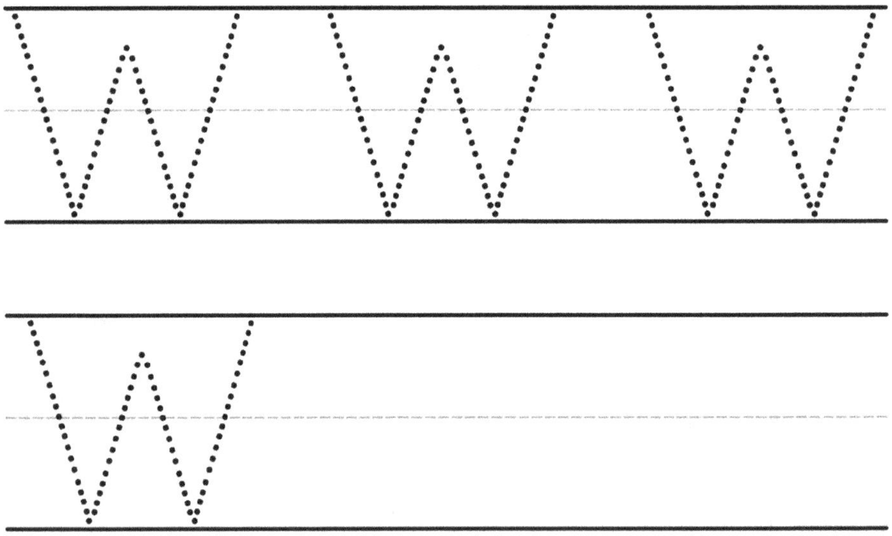

Trace the small alphabet

Look! The small 'w' is the <u>w</u>ind blowing hard! It's making the baby <u>w</u>olf feel cold in the <u>w</u>inter. Let's trace the 'w', so we can build a <u>w</u>arm den and keep the baby <u>w</u>olf cozy!

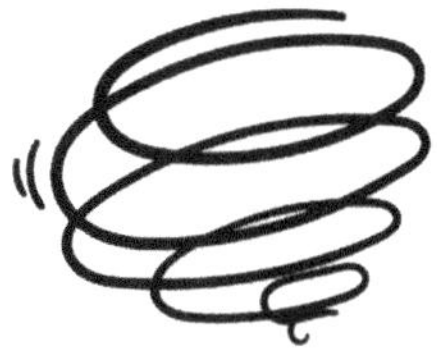

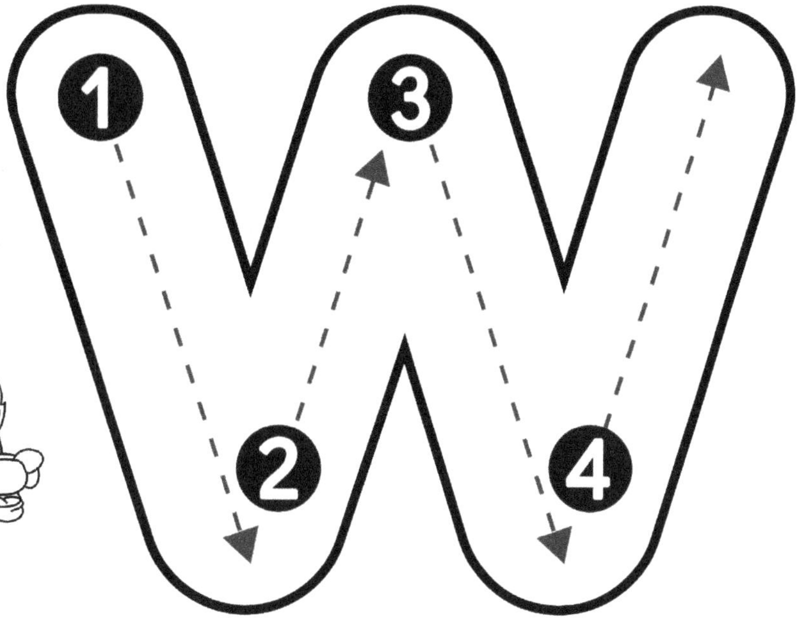

Time to Practice

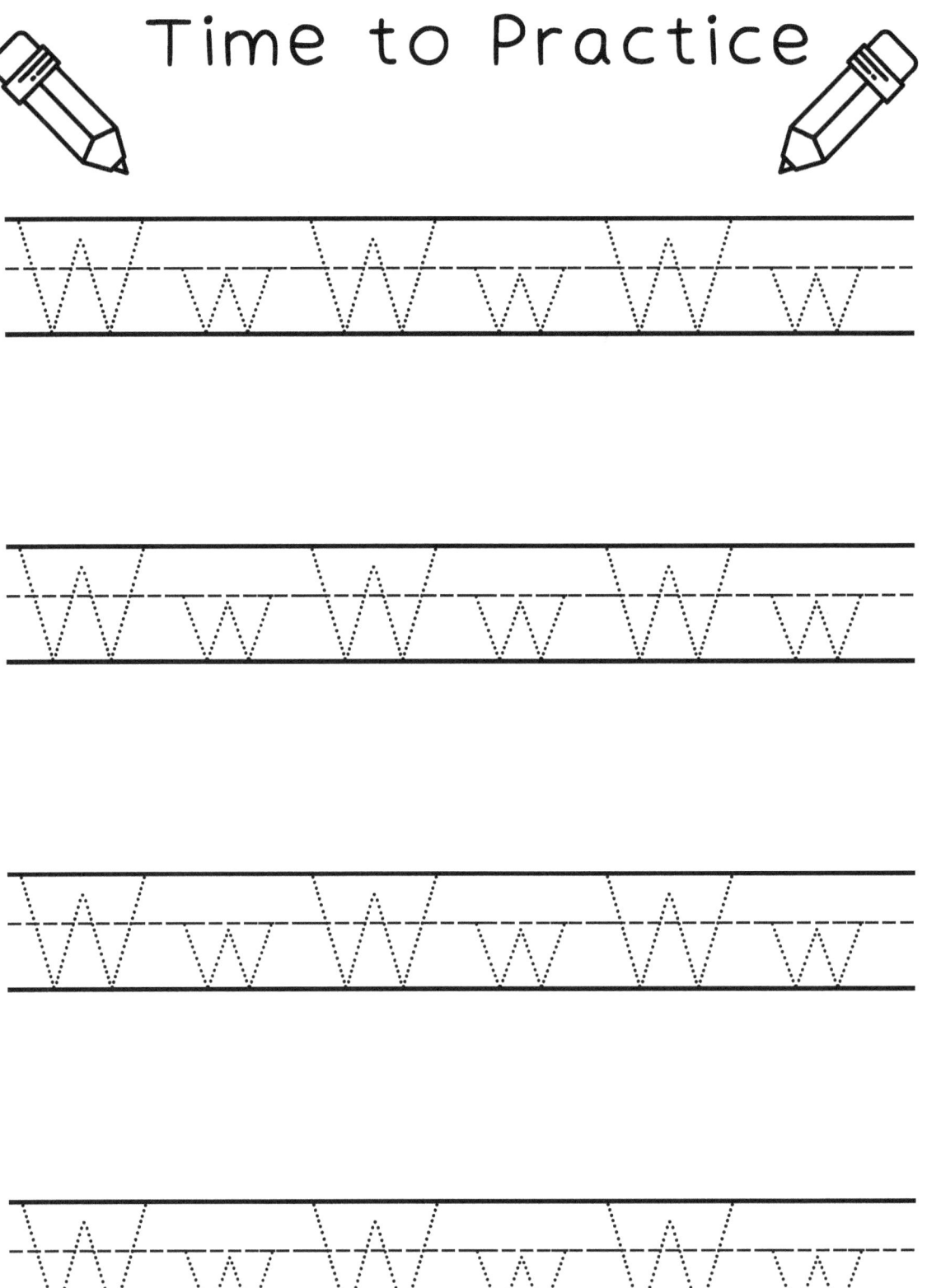

Color Me Fun!

<u>W</u>OW! You did a <u>w</u>onderful job tracing 'W'. Let's have some fun coloring <u>W</u>illy, the <u>w</u>hale.

W is for Whale

Did you Know? Whales sing songs underwater! They make all sorts of cool sounds that travel far through the ocean. Have you ever heard a whale?

Trace the X-tra Special X

 Look how special the 'X" looks because you are tracing it.

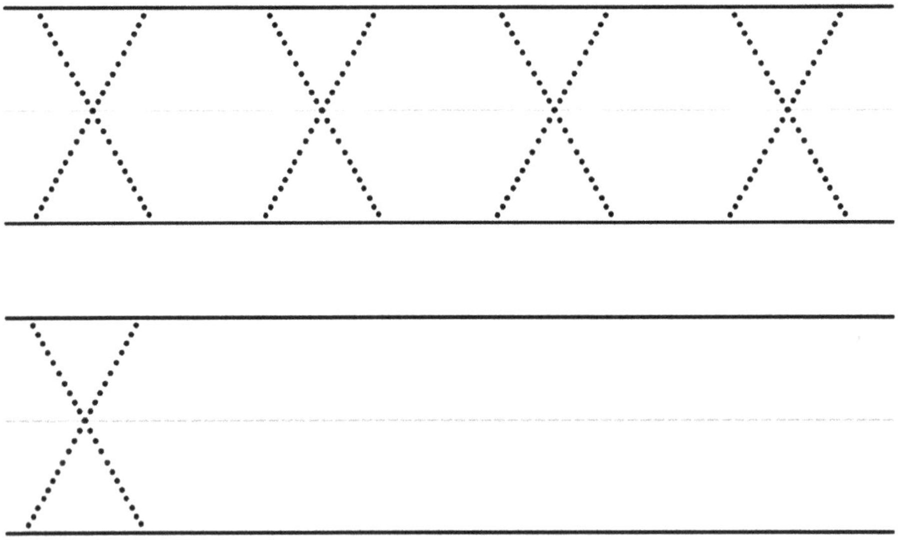

Trace the small alphabet

Look at those criss-cross lines. Can you use your super X-ray eyes to trace them like a master?

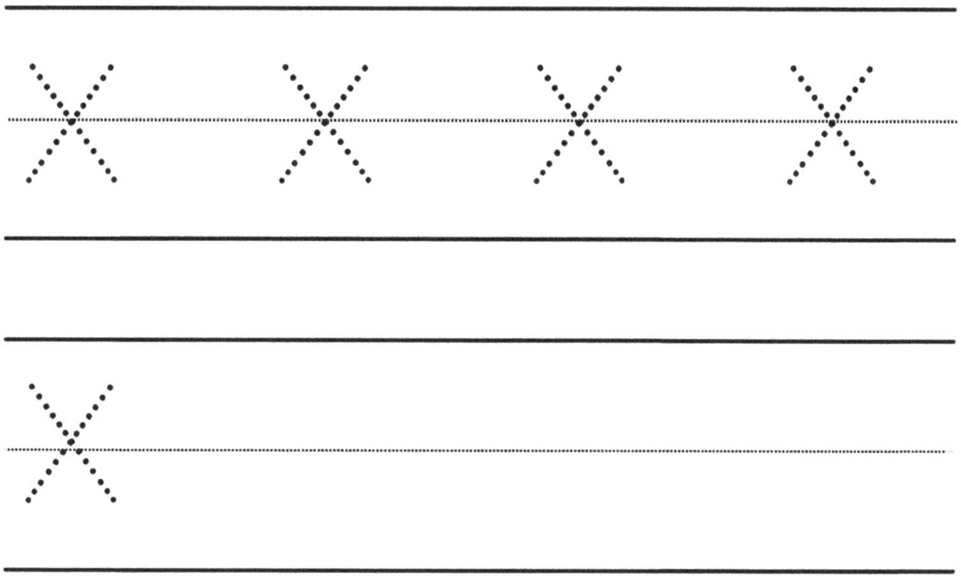

 # Time to Practice

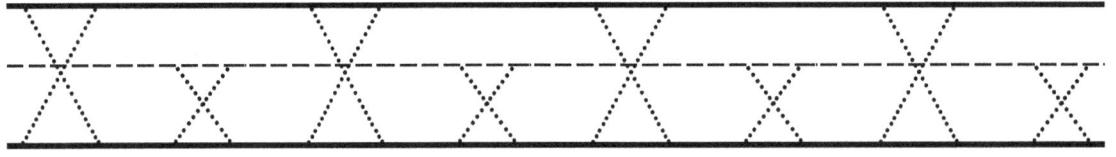

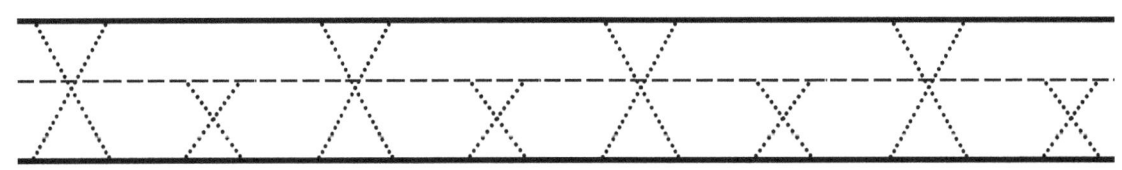

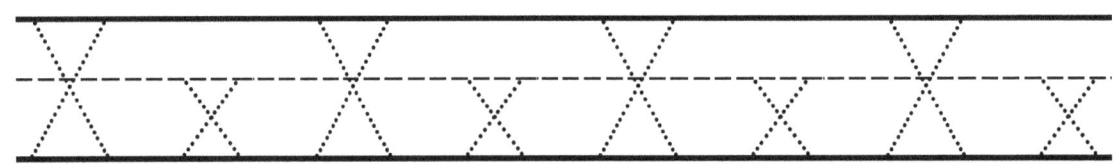

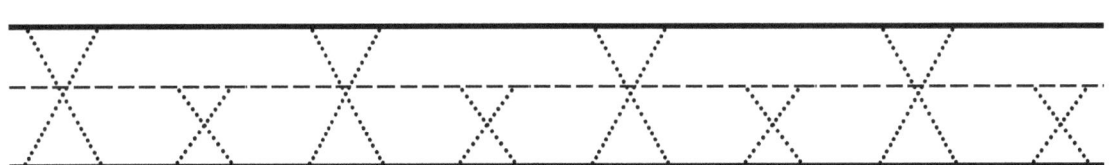

Color Me Fun!

 You did such a great job tracing 'X'. Now let's color the <u>xylophone</u> and make some beautiful music!

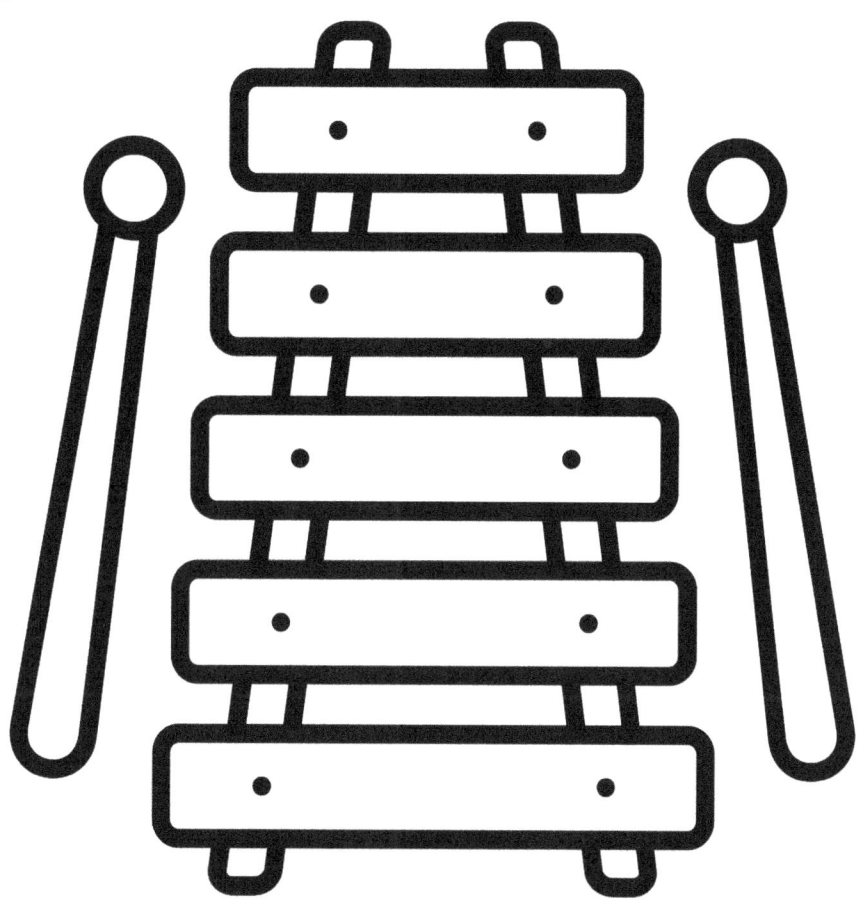

X is for xylophone
(xy-lo-phone)

Did you know? The xylophone is a musical instrument with lots of colorful bars!

Trace the Yummy Y

Let's trace that y̲ummy 'Y' and turn it into the y̲ummiest pretzel you've ever seen!

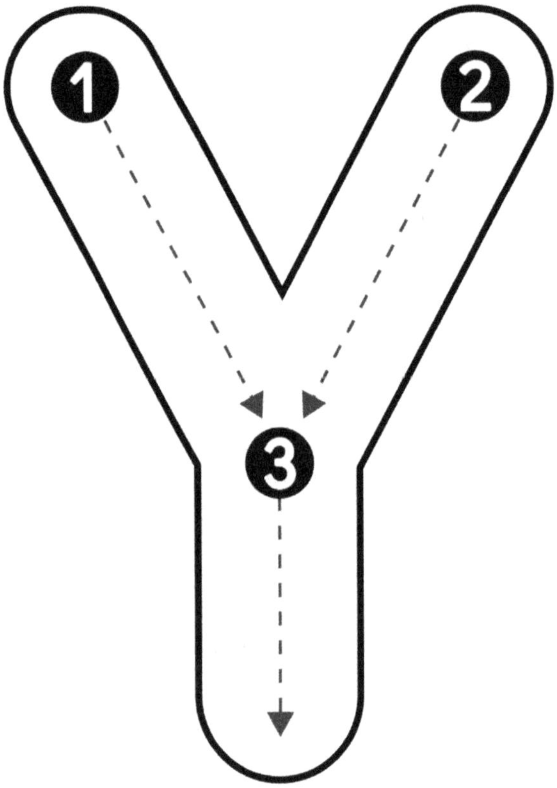

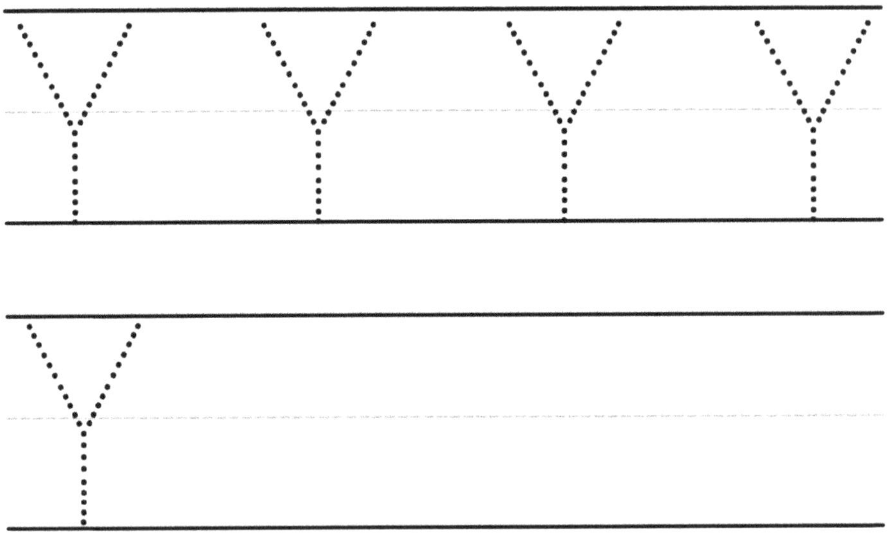

Trace the small alphabet

The small 'y' is feeling a little yellow today! Can you trace it to make it happy?

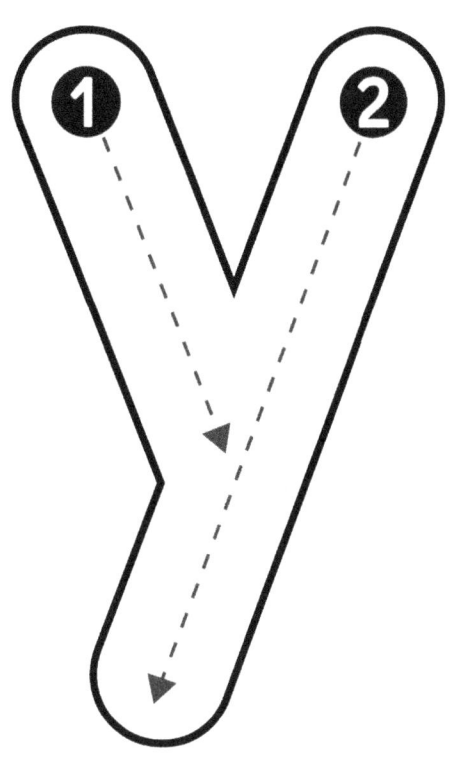

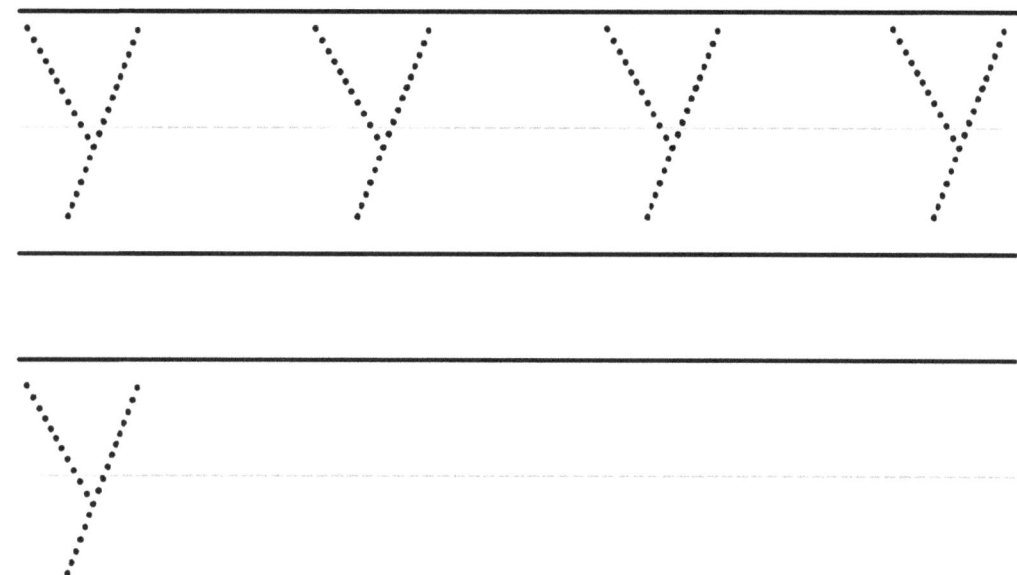

Time to Practice

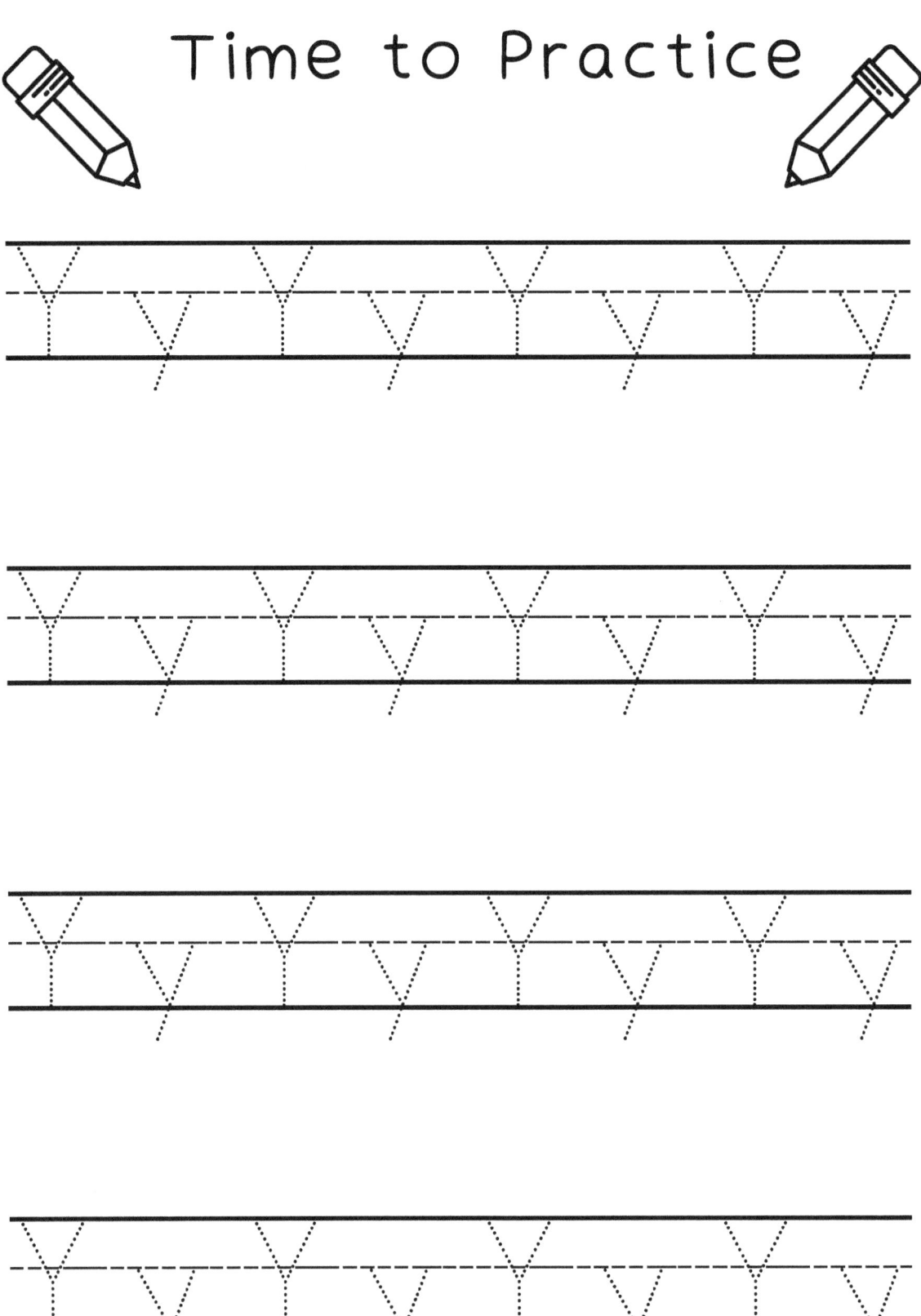

Color Me Fun!

Yippee! You were fantastic tracing 'Y'. Now, let's have lots of fun coloring Yoyo, the Yak.

Y is for Yak

Did you know? Yaks are super fluffy! Their fur is thick and warm, perfect for living in cold, snowy places.

Trace the Zig-Zag Z

Hey there, zookeeper! The path to the zoo is zig zag shaped! Can you trace it so all the animals can find their way in and play?

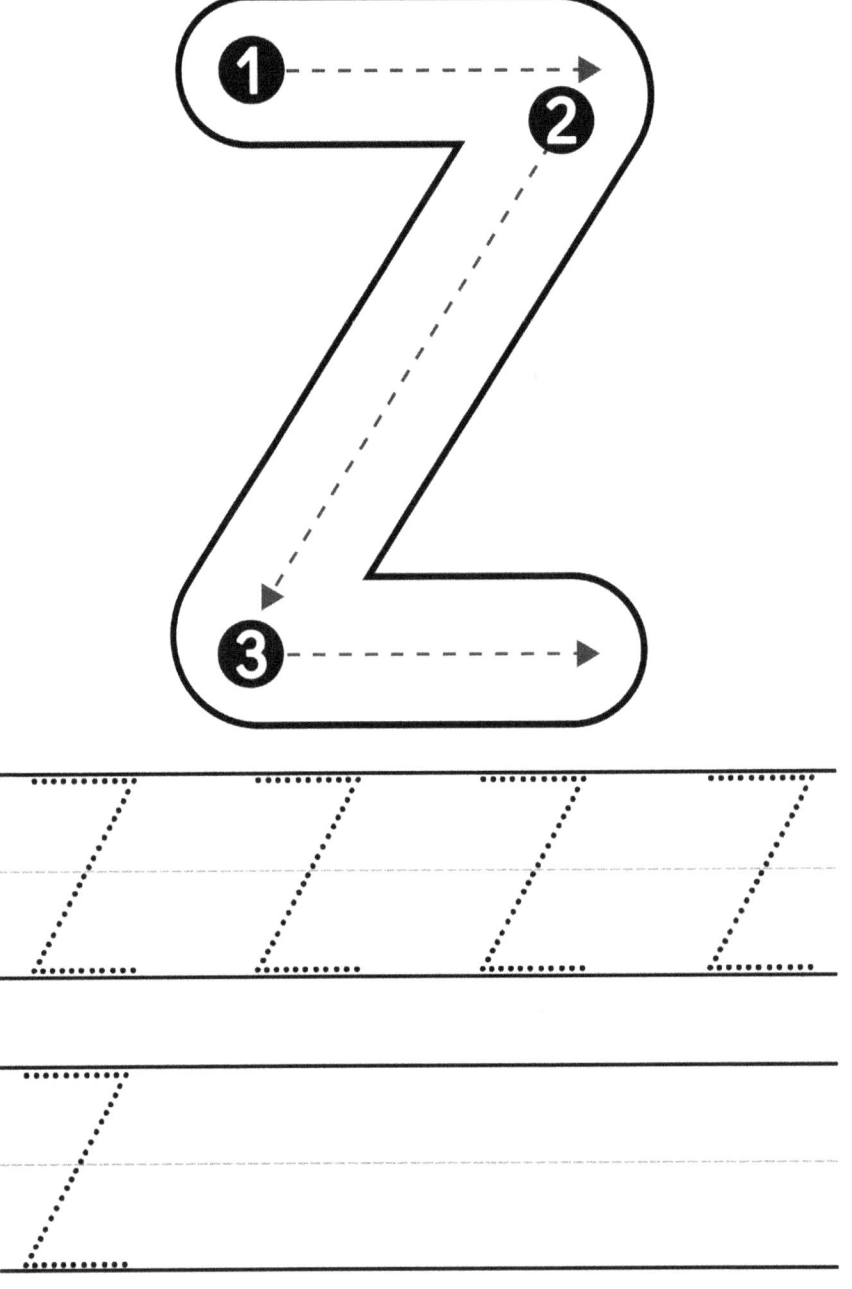

Trace the small alphabet

Look at that small 'z'! It wants to eat a big <u>z</u>ucchini to grow big and strong! Let's trace it and see if it grows!

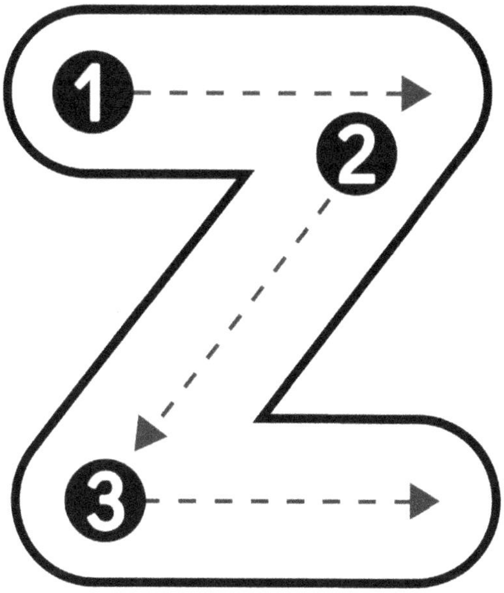

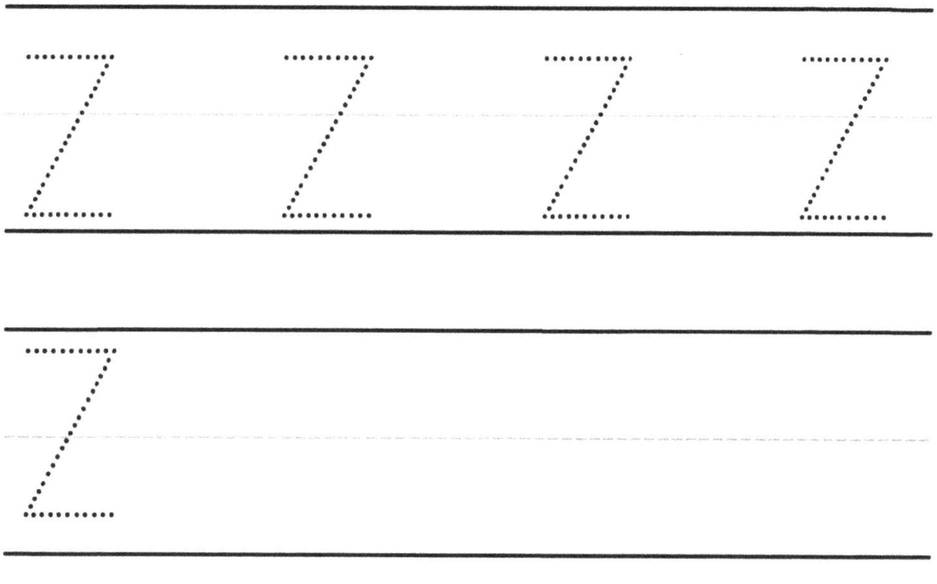

Time to Practice

Color Me Fun!

You're a zippy tracer! Ready to color the zebra's stripes.

Z is for Zebra

Did you know? Every zebra's stripes are different. No two zebras have exactly the same stripes.

Trace the lines

Trace the lines

Trace the lines

Trace the lines

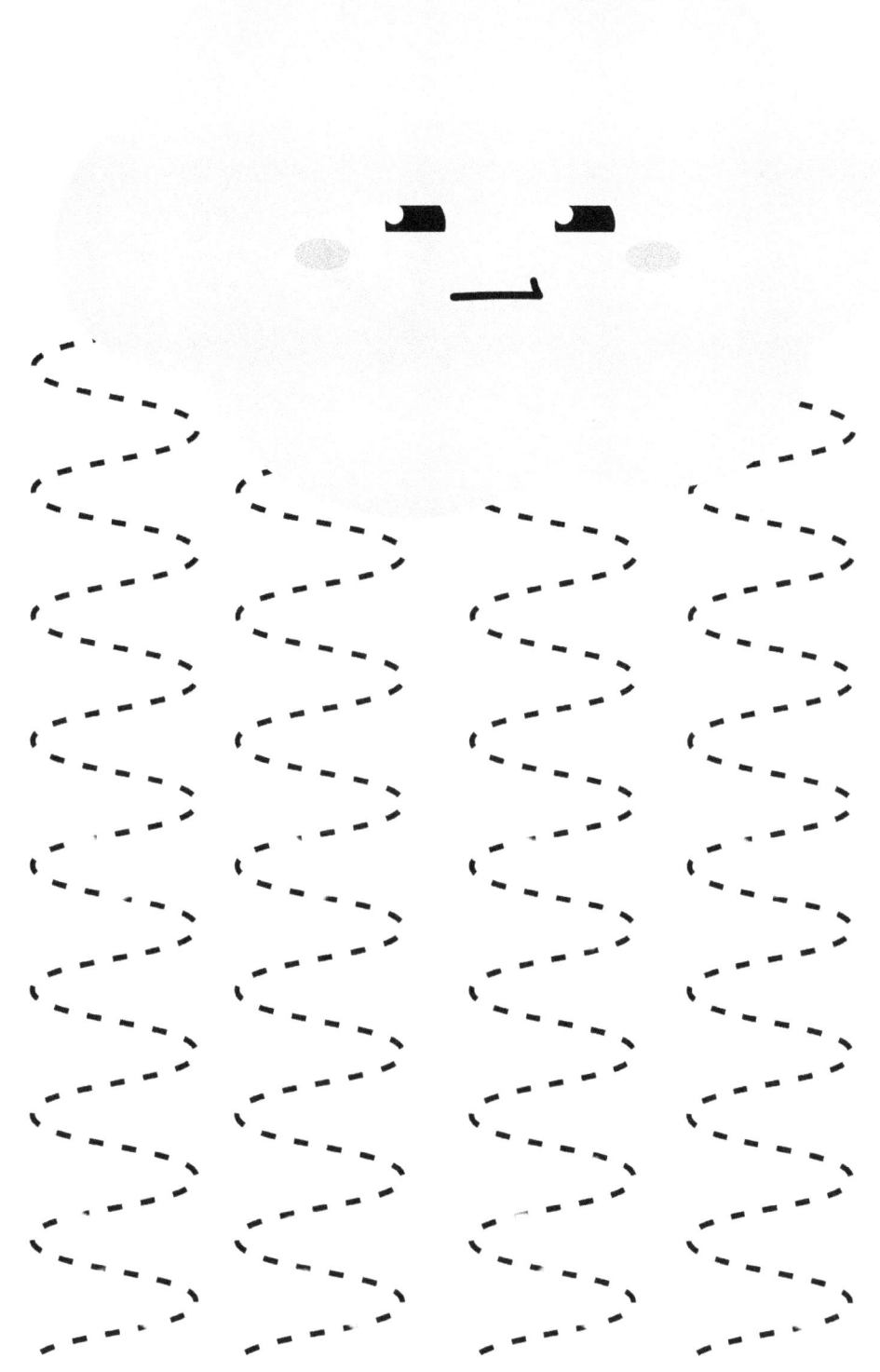

Trace the lines

Trace the lines

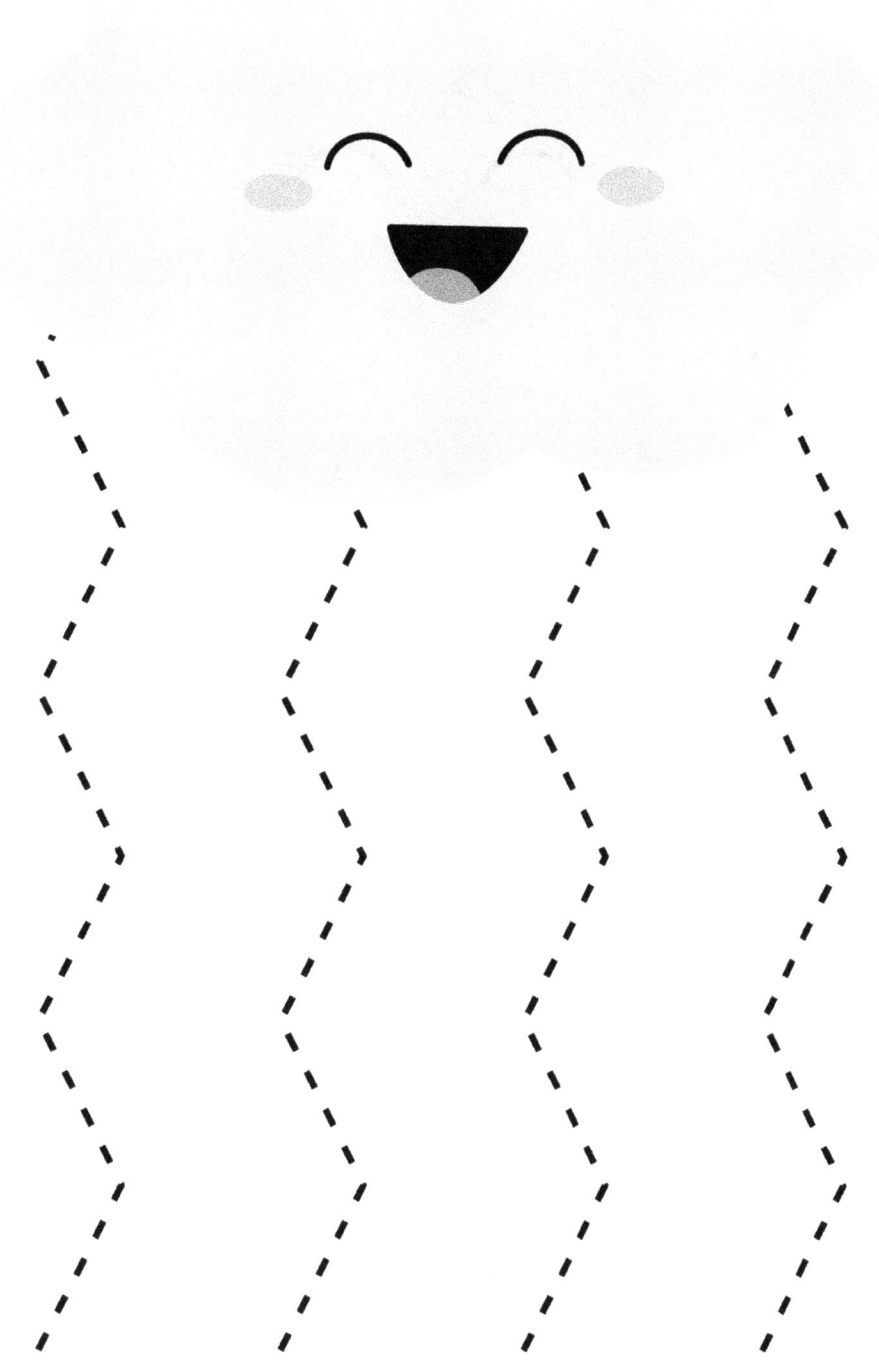

Trace the lines

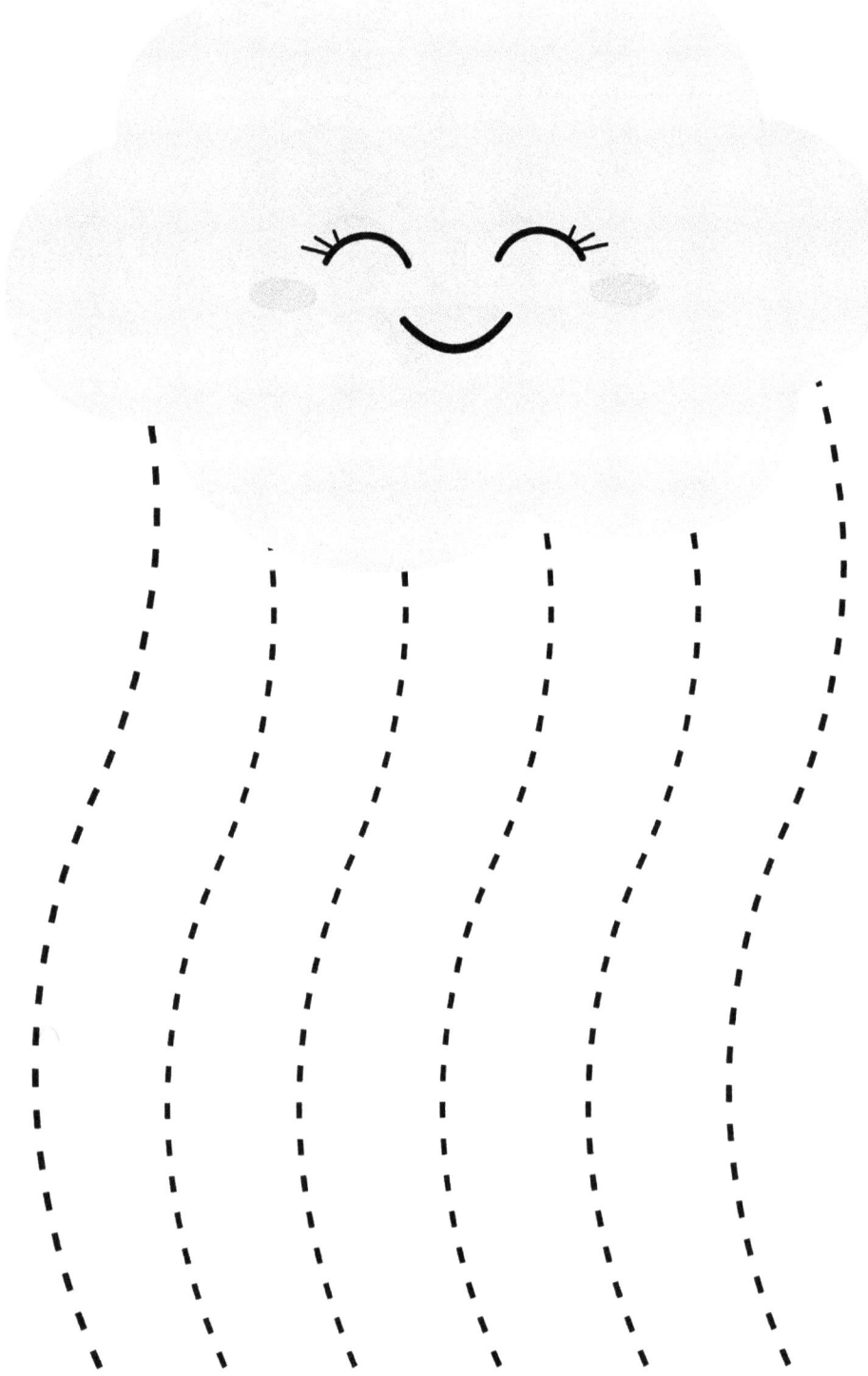

Trace the lines

Trace the lines

Trace the lines

Trace the lines

Wolly, the penguin is lost and needs to get home to his cozy igloo. Let's trace the zig zag lines to build a safe path for him to waddle all the way back!

Trace the lines

Trace the lines

Trace the lines

Trace the lines

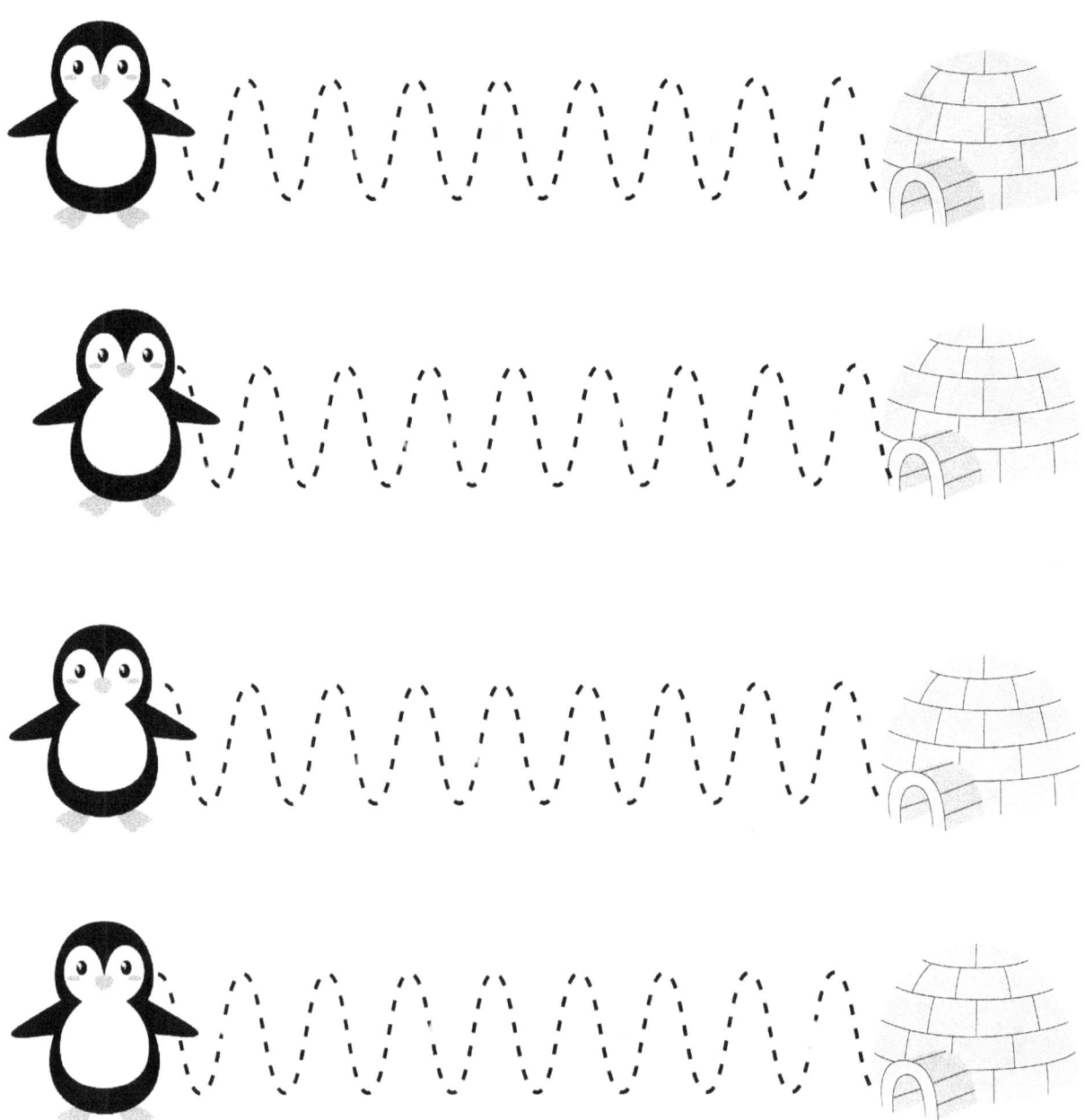

Trace the lines

Trace the lines

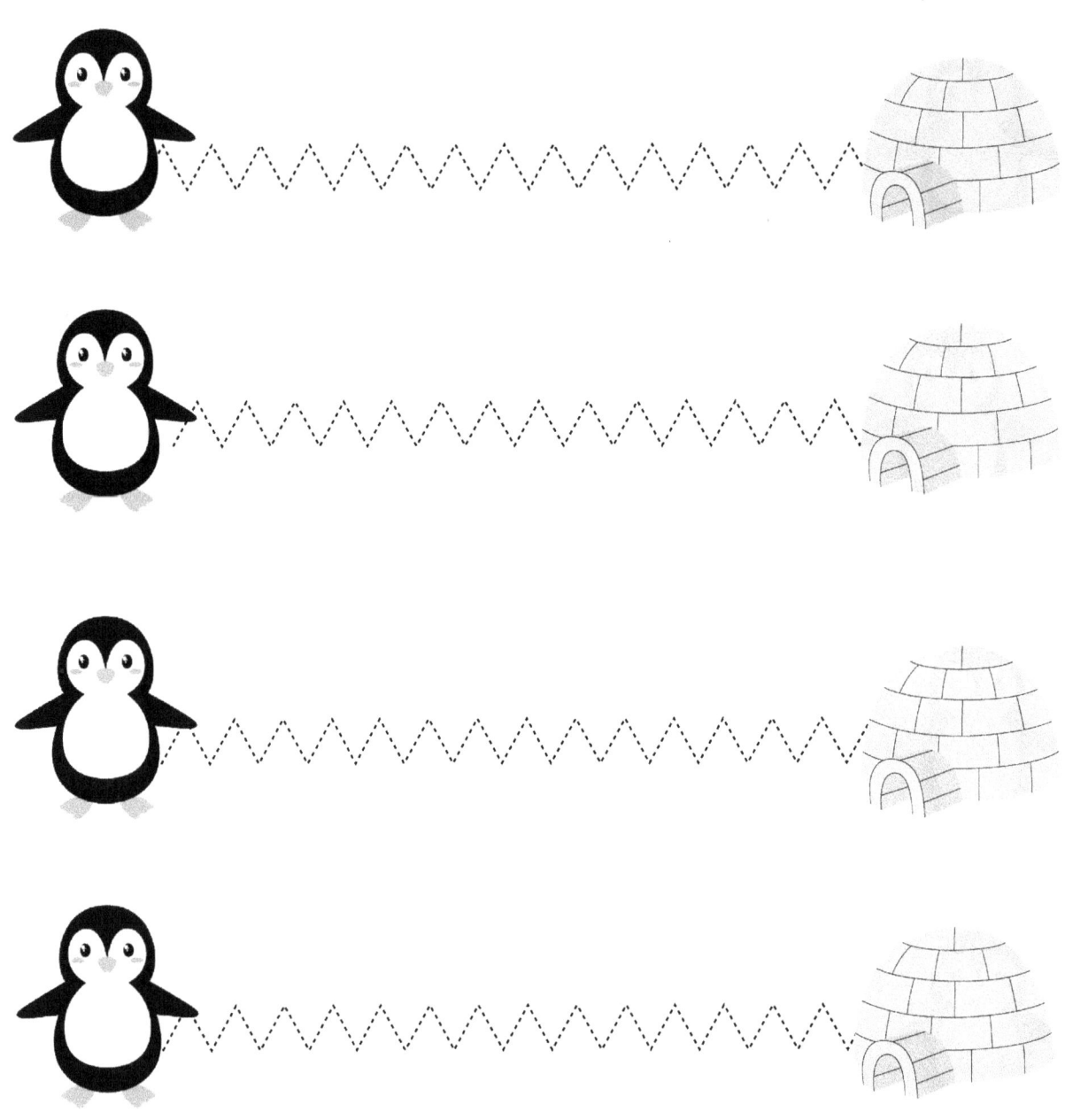

Trace the lines

Trace the lines

Trace the lines

Trace the numbers

Let's trace the number 1

Is the lamb big or small?

One

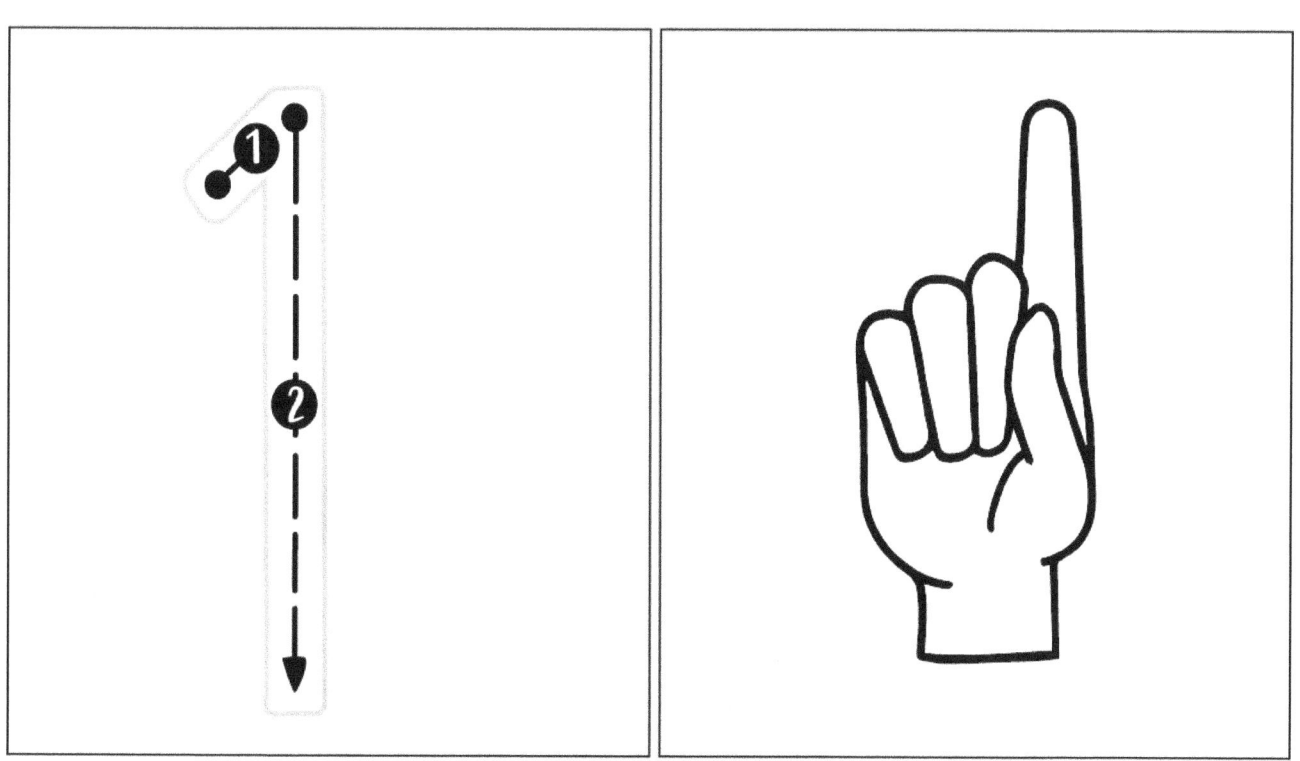

one

Trace Numbers

Let's trace the number 2

How many strawberries do you see?

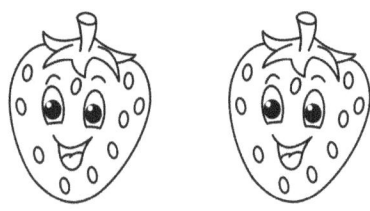

Two

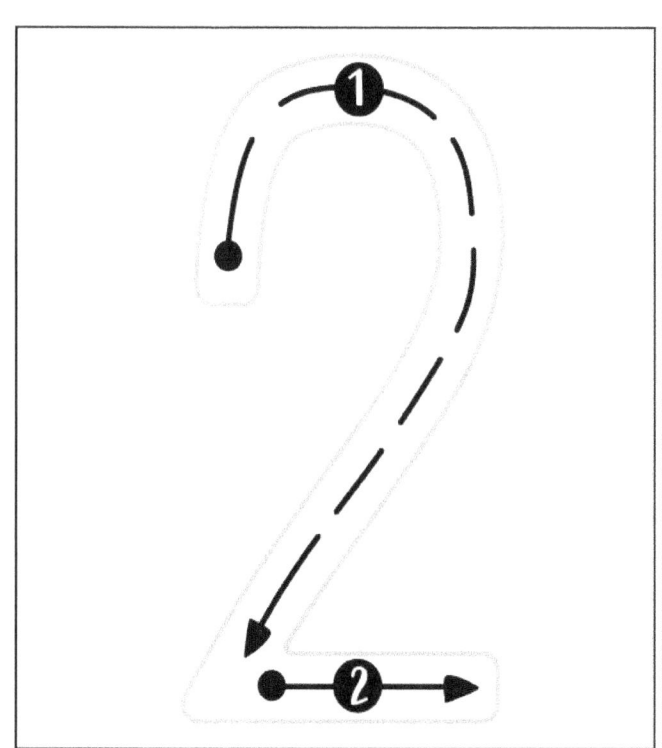

two

2 2 2 2 2

2 2 2 2 2

2 2 2 2 2

Trace Numbers

Let's trace the number 3

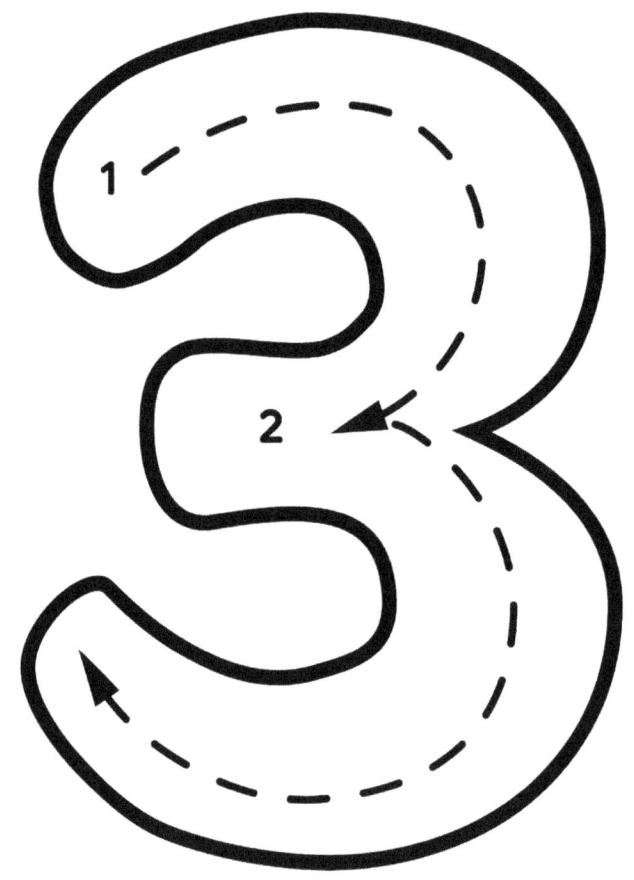

Look, there are 3 monkeys! What fun names can you give them?

Three

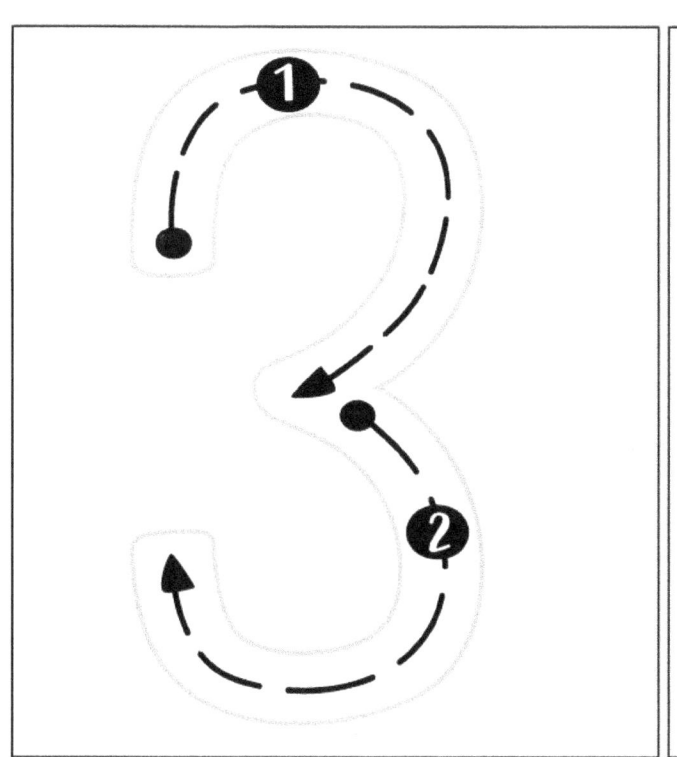

three

3 3 3 3 3

3 3 3 3 3

3 3 3 3 3

Trace Numbers

Let's trace the number 4

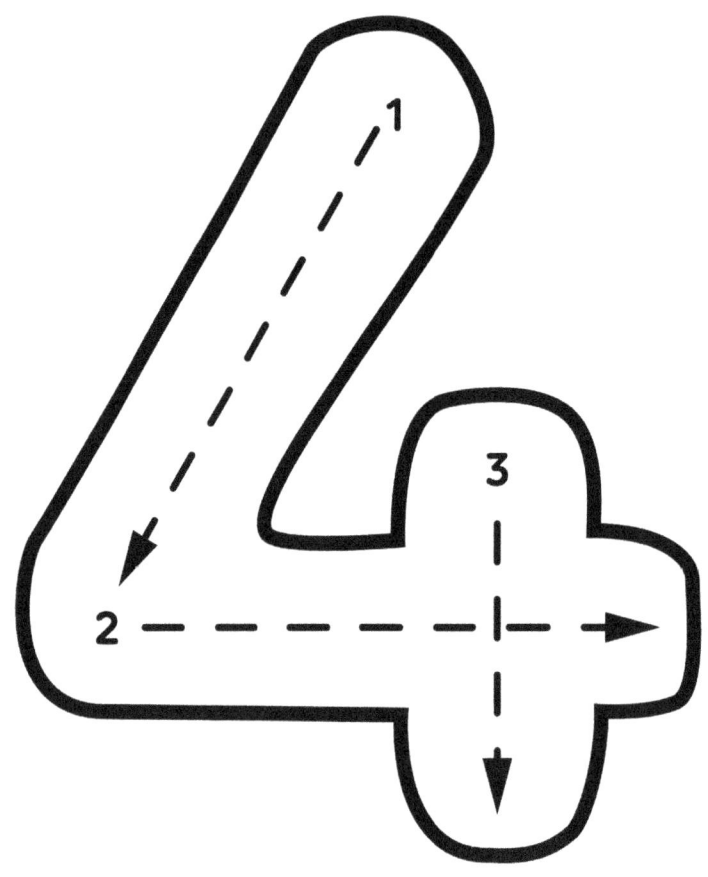

Look, there are 4 ducklings! Can you count them with your fingers?

Four

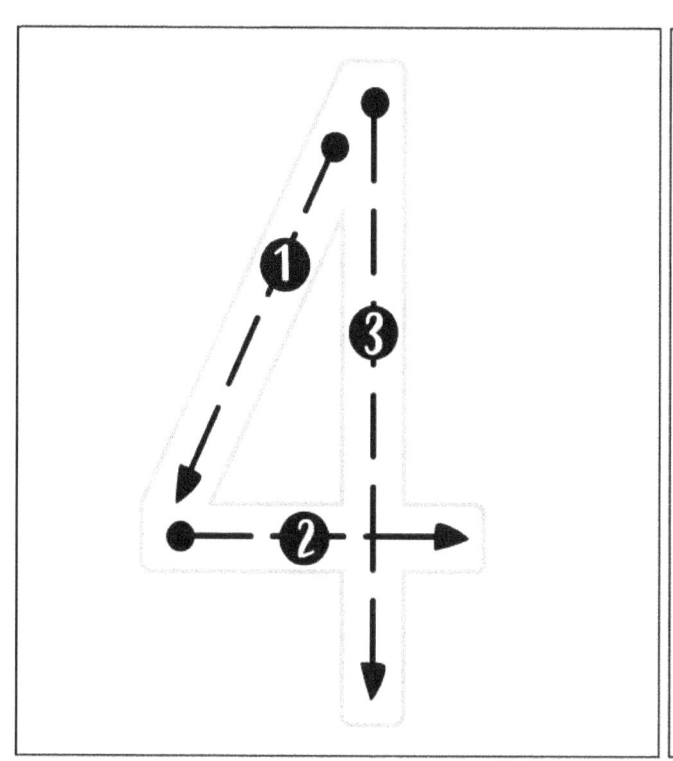
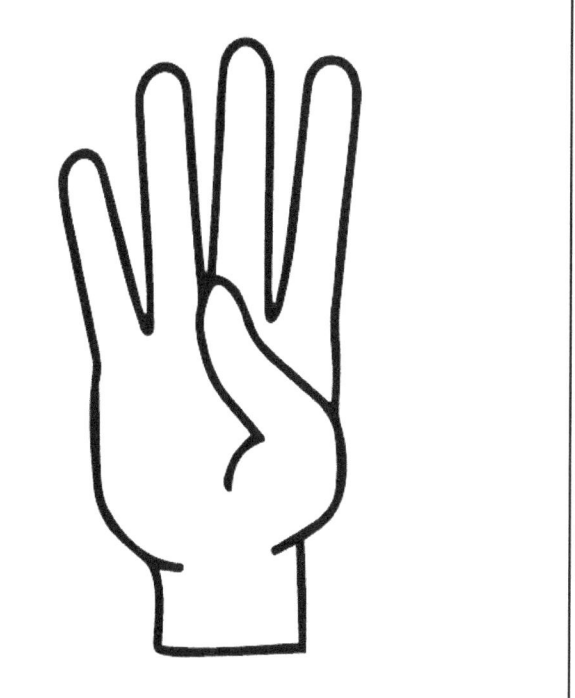

four

4 4 4 4 4

4 4 4 4 4

4 4 4 4 4

Trace Numbers

Let's trace the number 5

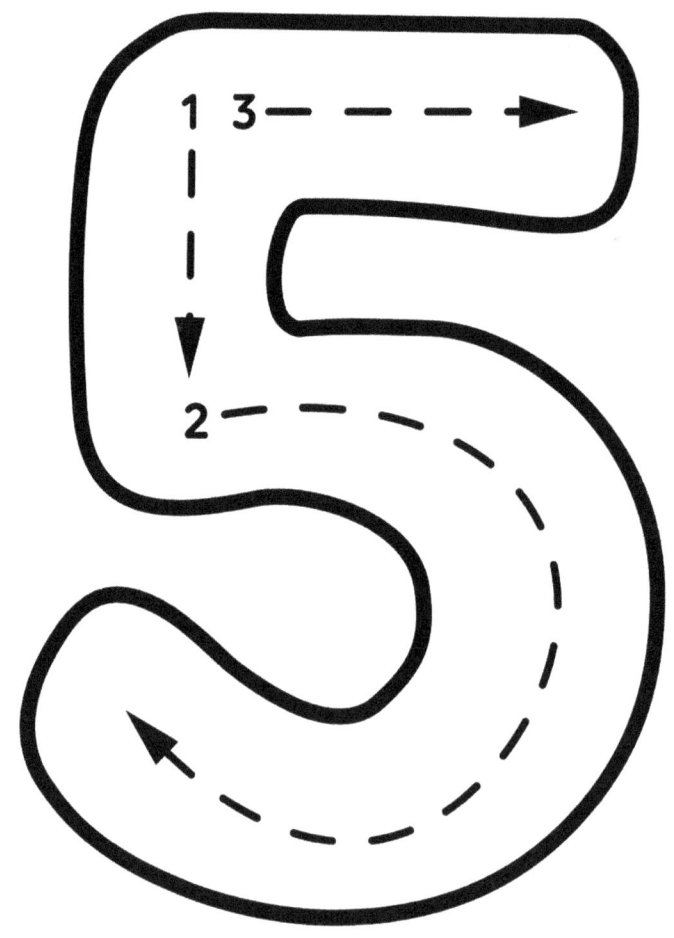

Baa like a sheep 5 times!

Five

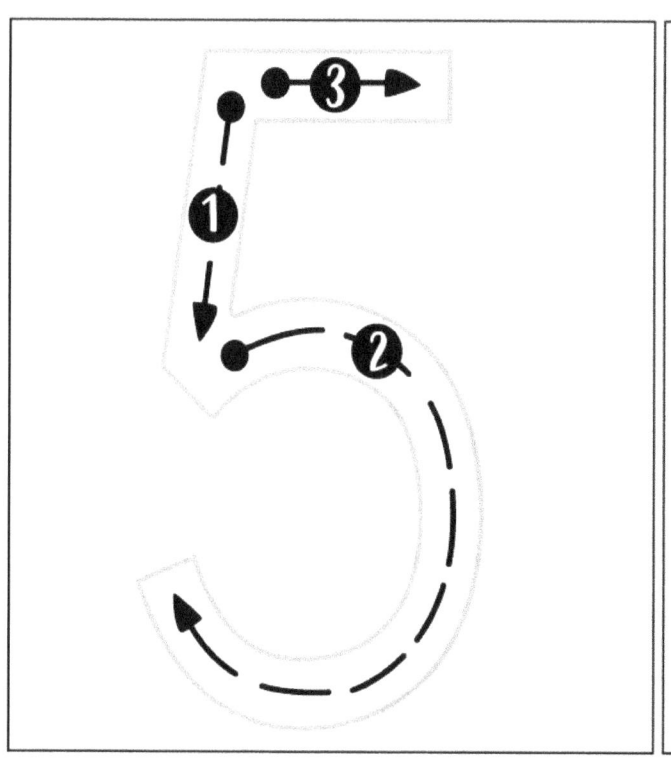

five

Trace Numbers

Let's trace the number 6

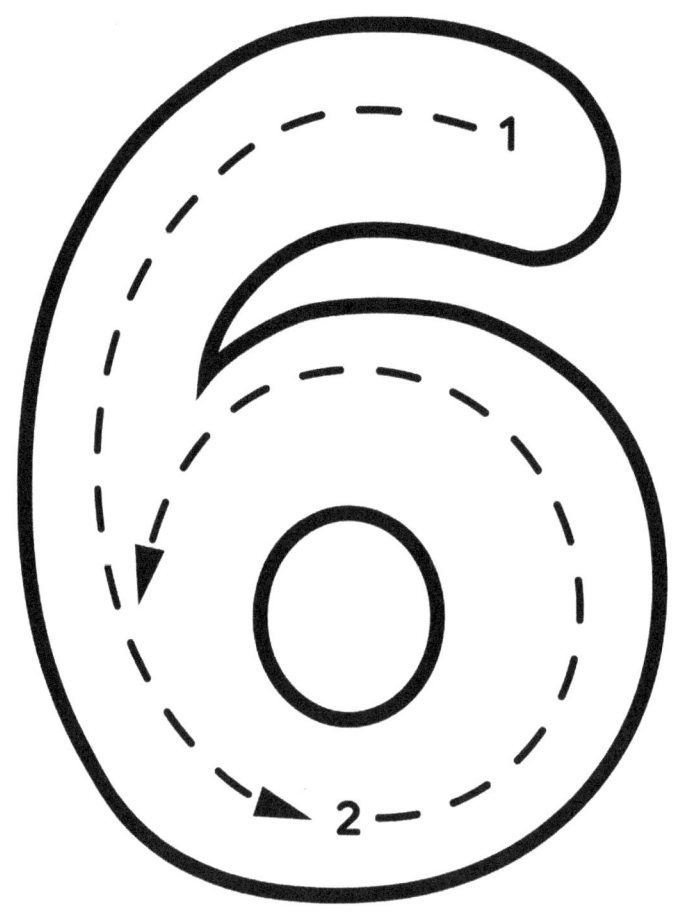

Let's count the camels using our fingers. How many camels are there?

Six

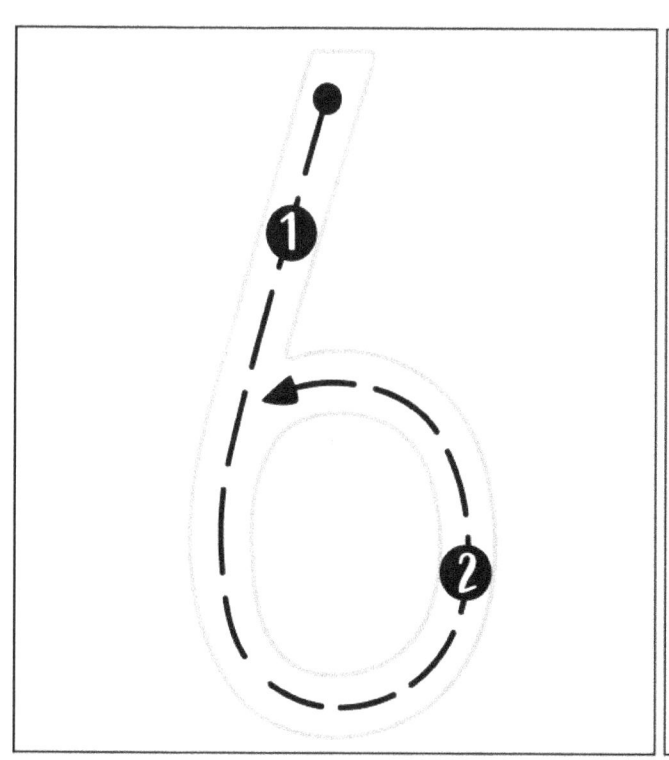
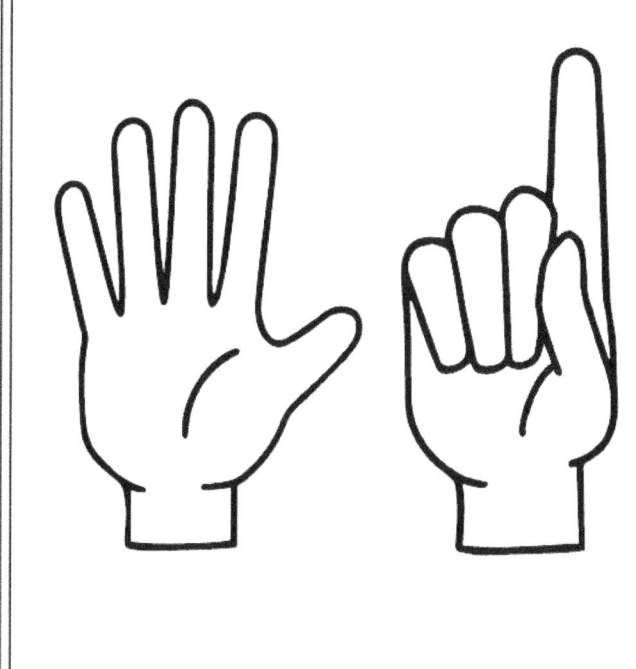

six

6 6 6 6 6

6 6 6 6 6

6 6 6 6 6

Trace Numbers

Let's trace the number 7

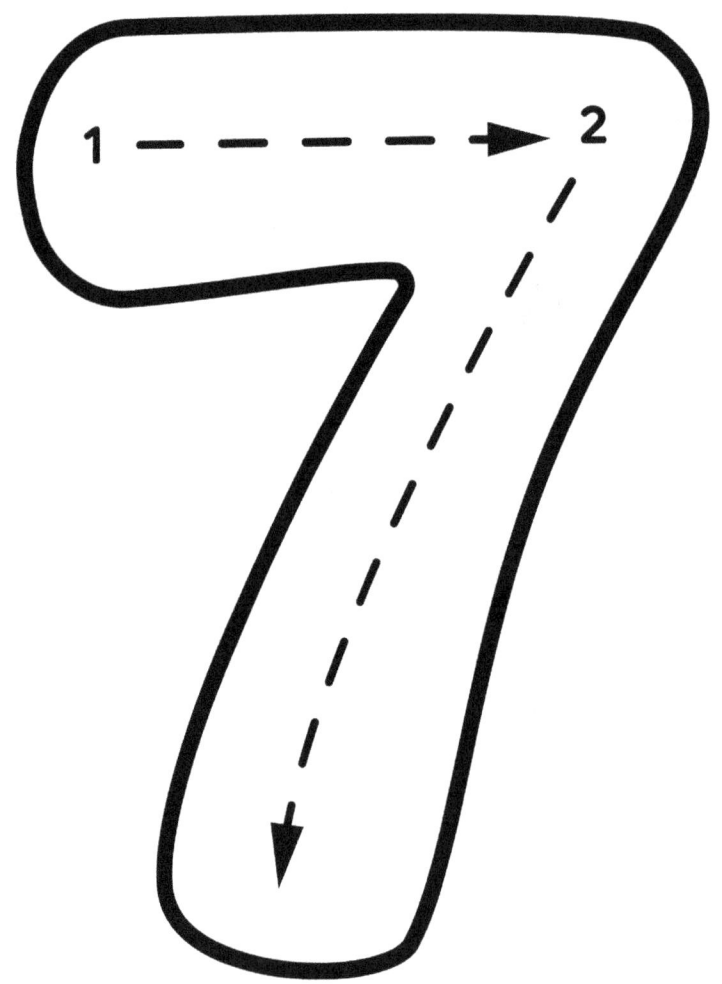

The 7 rabbits are all ready to go to a carrot party. Let's count them one by one so we don't miss them.

seven

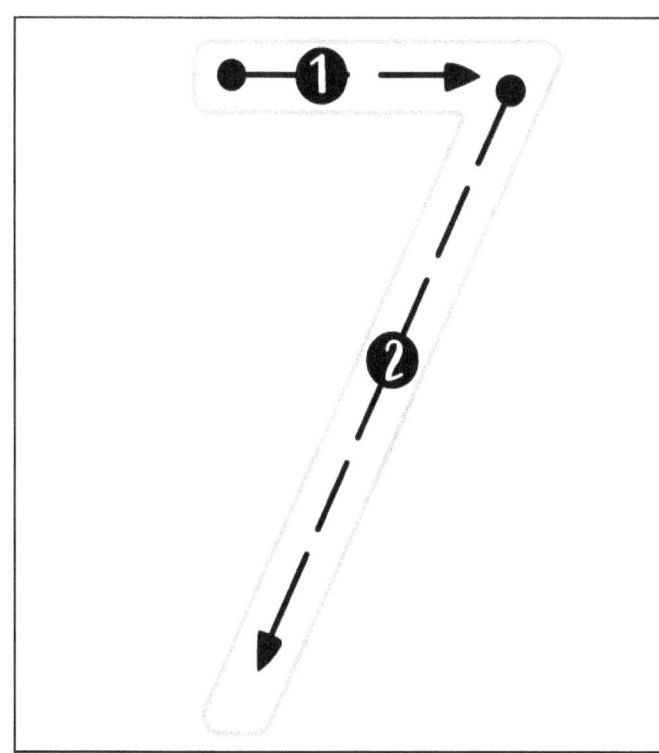

seven

Trace Numbers

Let's trace the number 8

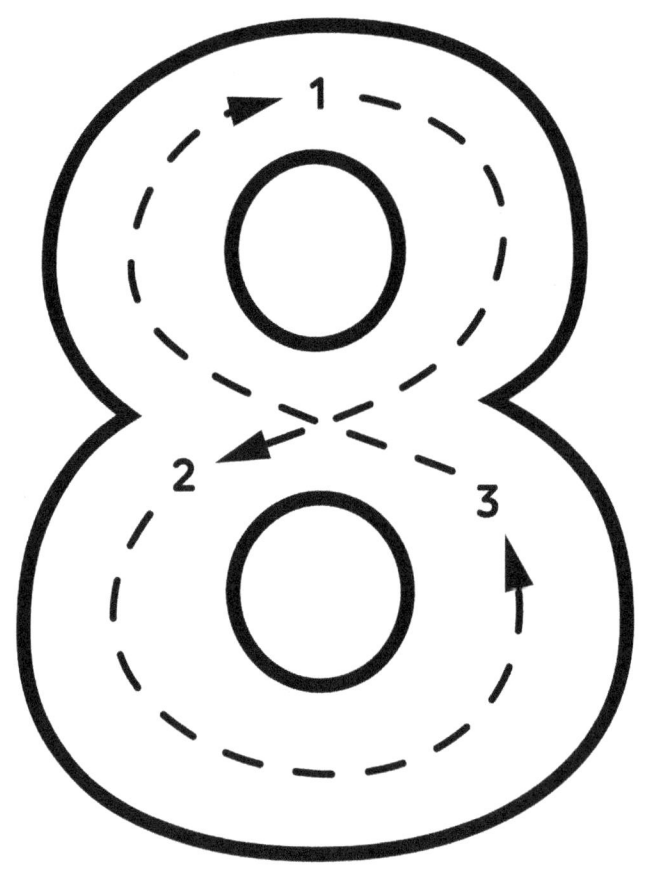

Look at all the yummy apples! How many can you pick today!

Eight

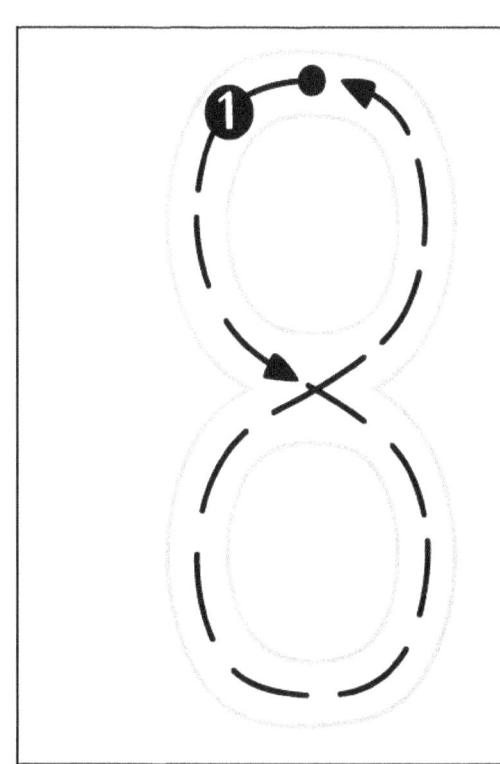
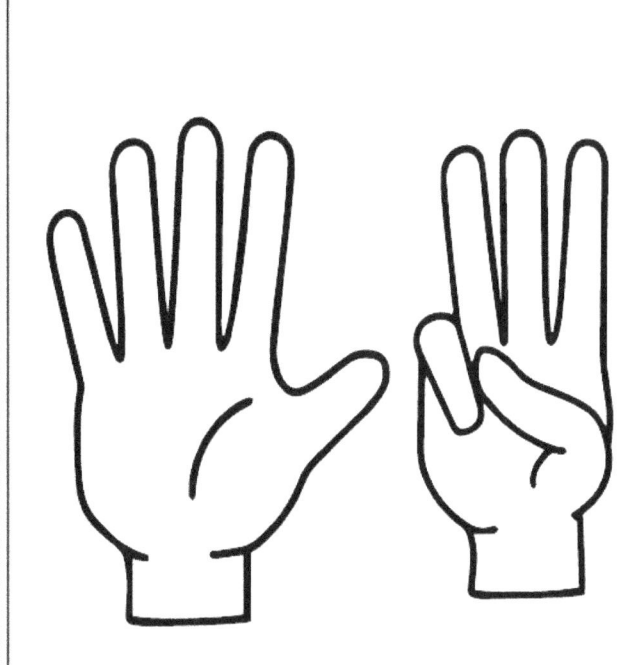

eight

8
8
8

Trace Numbers

Let's trace the number 9

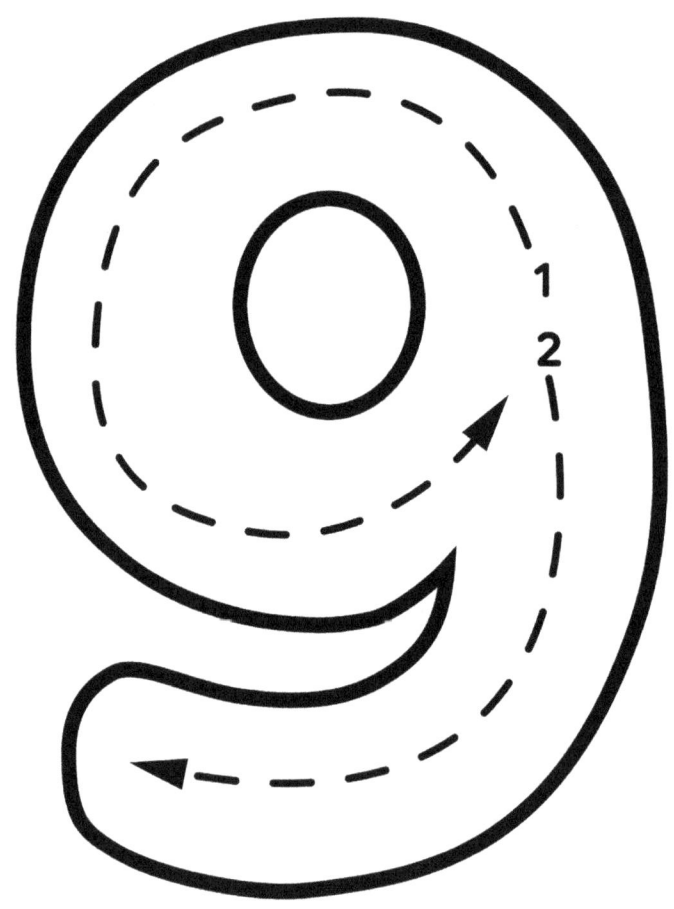

Let's pretend to be a fish! Can you use your hand to swim around like the fish 9 times.

Nine

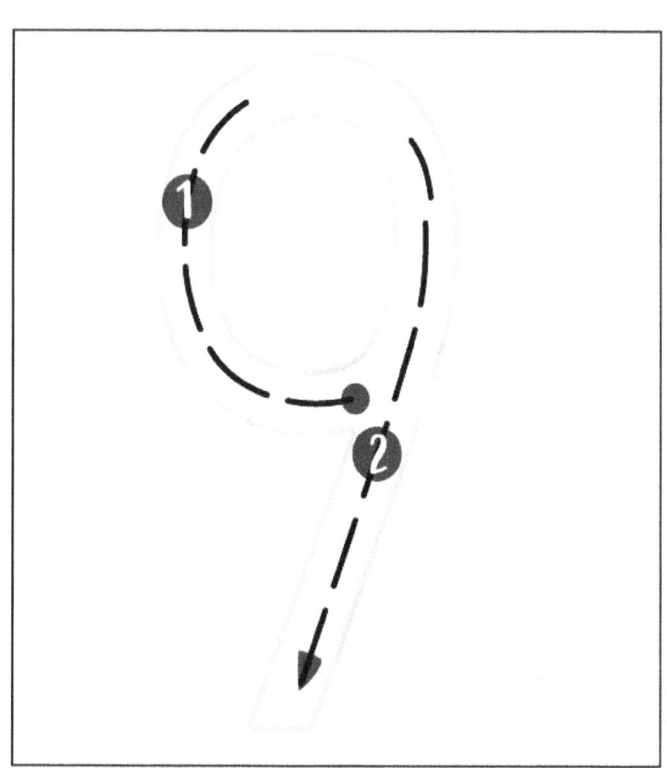
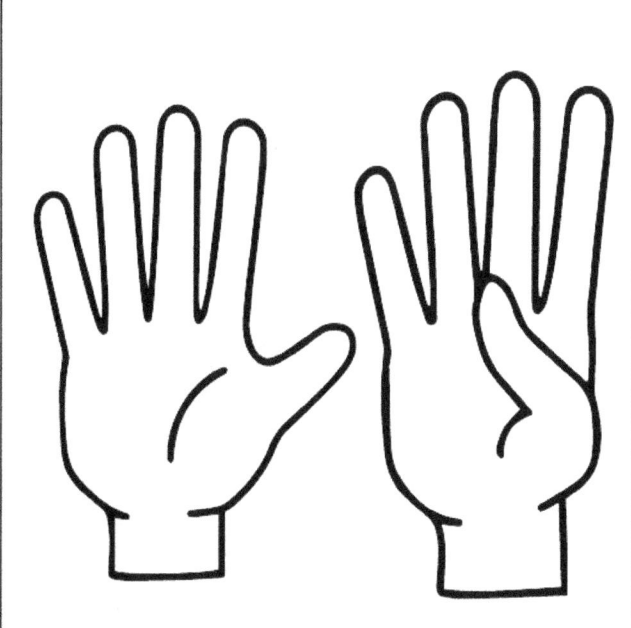

nine

9
9
9

Trace Numbers

Let's trace the number 10

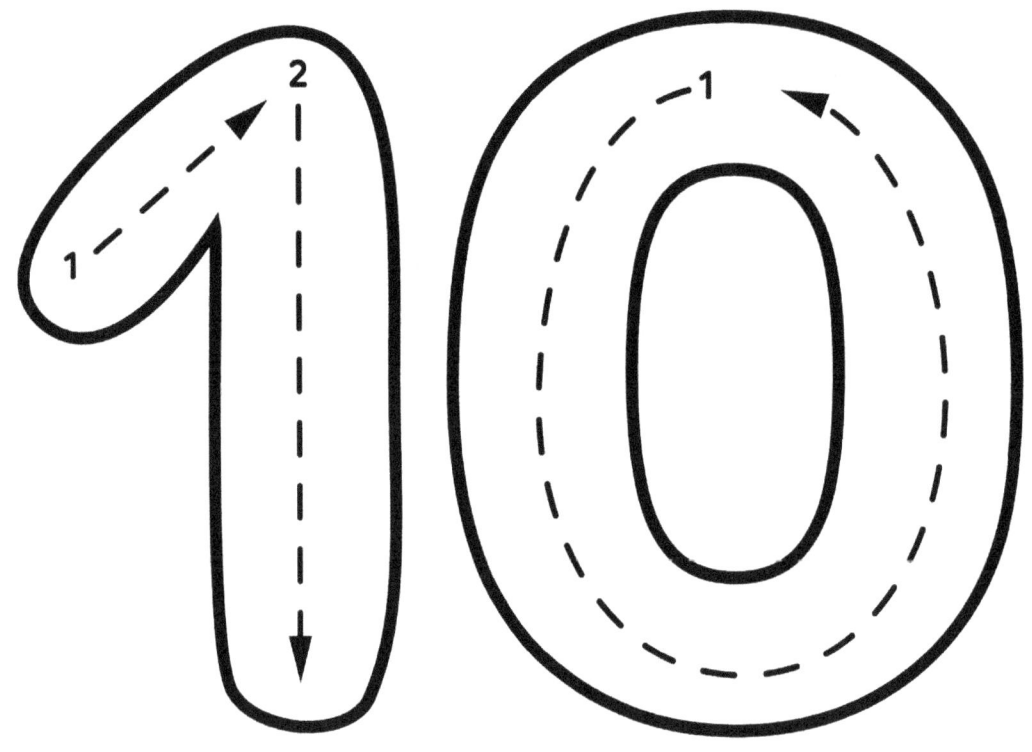

Picnic time for ladybugs! How many are sharing a meal? Let's count!

Ten

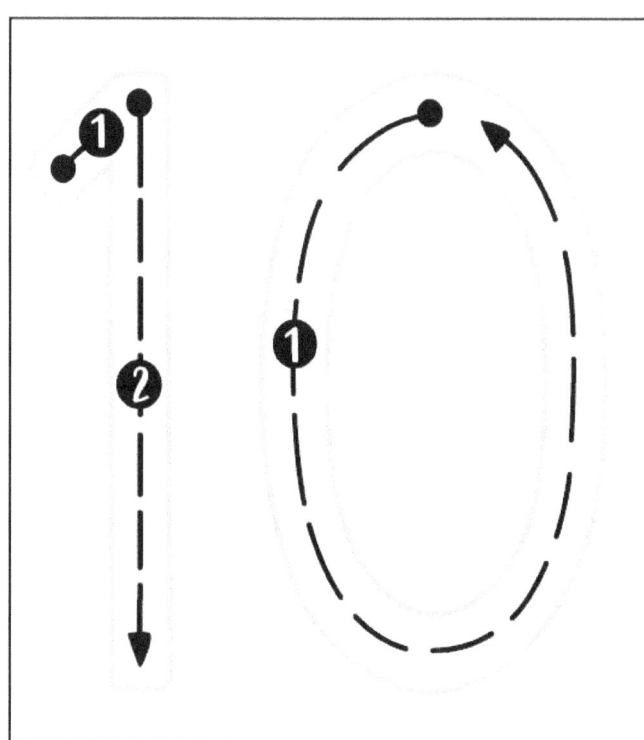

ten

10 10 10 10

10 10 10 10

10 10 10 10

Trace the Shapes

Color the moon blue.
Color the star yellow.
Color the heart red.

Trace the Shapes

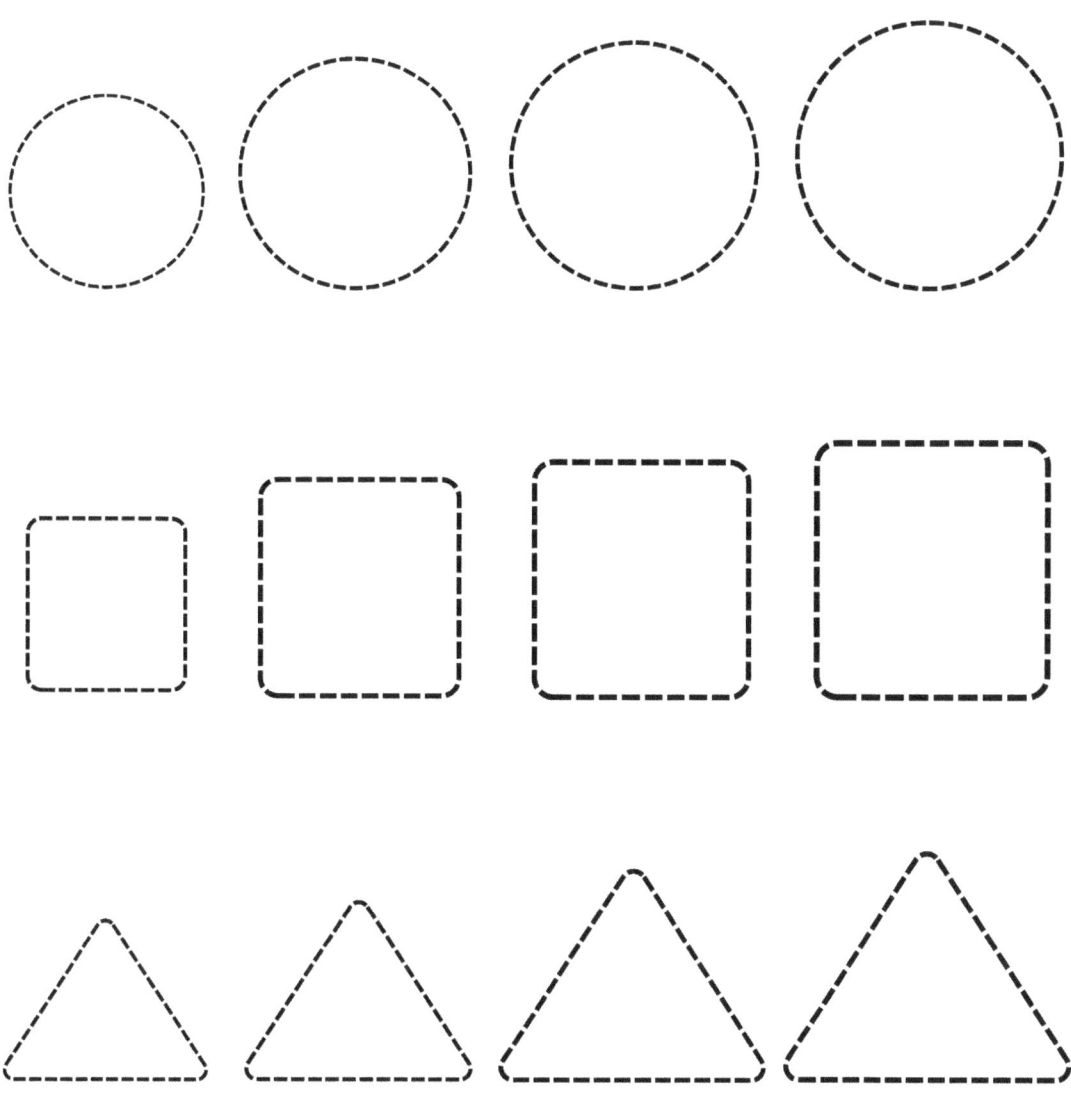

Color the circle ◯ orange.
Color the square ☐ purple.
Color the triangle △ brown.

Trace the Squares

Trace the Circles

Trace the Triangles

Let's find the shapes

Look at these yummy cookies! Circle the cookie that looks like a circle with your favorite crayon!

Look at these fun shapes! Circle the shape that has four equal sides like a gift box with your favorite crayon.

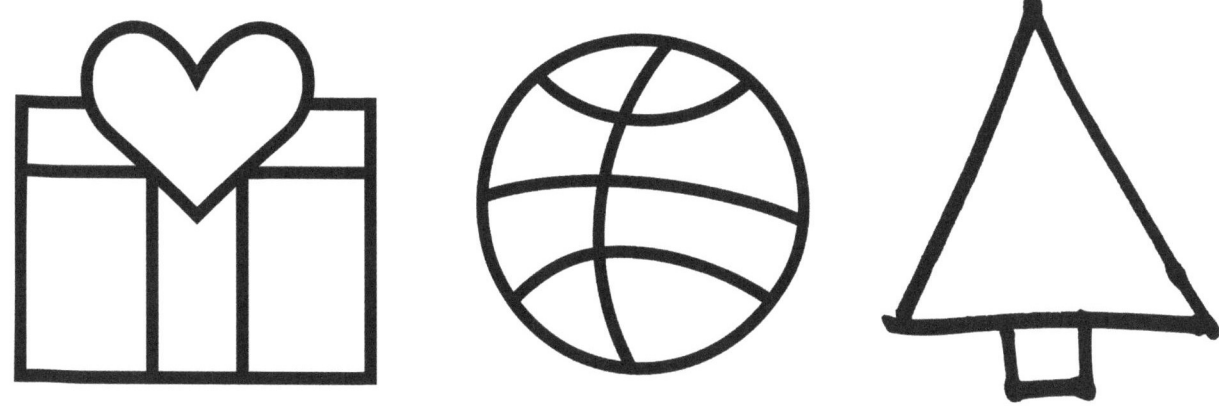

Let's find the shapes

Which one is round like a ball - the sun or the pointy building? Circle the round one with your crayon!

Look at these shapes! Circle the one that has pointy corners like a slice of pizza?

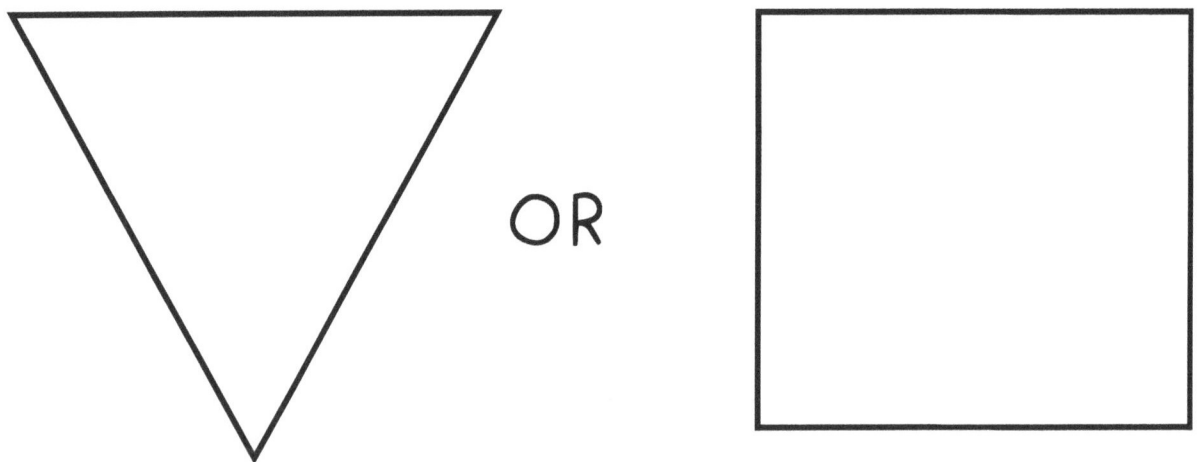

Congratulations!

Certificate Of Achievement
Tracing Champion

This Certificate is proudly presented to:

_____

for their outstanding achievement in tracing alphabets, shapes, and numbers.

_____
Date

www.ingramcontent.com/pod-product-compliance
Lightning Source LLC
Chambersburg PA
CBHW081323040426
42453CB00013B/2289